fuckless

Gianna Biscontini, MA EdHD, BCBA

fuckless

A Guide to Wild,
Unencumbered
Freedom

DYNAMITE LADY
PUBLISHING

FUCKLESS

A Guide to Wild, Unencumbered Freedom

FIRST EDITION

ISBN   978-1-5445-3045-1 *Hardcover*
       978-1-5445-3046-8 *Paperback*
       978-1-5445-3047-5 *Ebook*
       978-1-5445-3048-2 *Audiobook*

I wholeheartedly believe in the power every woman has to evolve her own life by conscious endeavor. I wrote this book in the service of all women, to help liberate them from generations of limiting narratives and rules on what it means to be female. Authenticity for women is not perfection; it's learning to show up and own the messy, cracked, gorgeous-in-all-our-glory versions of ourselves. The woman we hide but know is there. The person we'll look back on when we're seventy and say, "I wish I hadn't hidden that lovely, fierce girl for so long."

While I've known many lovely, fierce females over the course of my life, this book would never have been written without inspiration from a special few:

To Glennon Doyle and Megan Rapinoe, who gave me permission to be wild. To Ruth Bader Ginsberg, who showed me that a polarizing but industrious quiet can be powerful too. And to my tenacious, free-spirited rescue pup, Olivia Chewton John, who taught me to always, forever, and no matter what—just keep living.

Contents

BEFORE DIVING IN... 11

DARK CAVES AND OH SHIT MOMENTS.........................19

FUCK. THIS. 29

PART ONE: THE FUCKS WE'RE GIVEN

1. BE SMALL..43

   FUCK BEING SMALL..59

2. BE SOFT 63

   FUCK BEING SOFT..83

3. BE LESS 87

   FUCK BEING LESS 105

4. BE THE EXCEPTION..109

   FUCK BEING THE EXCEPTION.......................................123

5. BE STIFLED 127

   FUCK BEING STIFLED 139

6. BE EVERYTHING 143

   FUCK BEING EVERYTHING 155

7. BE CHOSEN 159

FUCK BEING CHOSEN 177

8. BE DEPENDENT 181

FUCK BEING DEPENDENT 193

9. BE FIXED 197

FUCK BEING FIXED 213

10. BE SEXY...BUT SWEET 217

FUCK BEING SEXY...BUT SWEET 247

INTERMISSION BRAIN BREAK 251

PART TWO: LIVING (AND STAYING) FUCK-FREE

SHOW YOU WHAT YOU'RE MADE OF 255

IDENTIFYING VALUES.............................. 269

ENERGY REDISTRIBUTION 273

WEIGHING ALTERNATIVES 275

LANGUAGE SIGNALS 277

REGIFTING...279

CREATE THE OPEN DOOR......................... 283

CELEBRATE.. 287

GO ON, *GLOW*.................................... 289

APPENDIX: REINFORCEMENT AND PUNISHMENT 297

Fuckless (adj.):

Delightfully liberated from the fears, opinions, beliefs, desires, and/ or expectations of others.

See also: free, unaffected, sovereign.

Before
Diving In...

What I've learned in my nearly twenty-year career as a behavior scientist is that people are varying degrees of fascinated with the research on why we do what we do. My goal here is to light you up from the inside so you can rethink your beliefs and change the way you show up in the world. That's hard to do if you, dear reader, are bored.

If you're a nerd like me, you might want to know exactly what publications I'm referencing when I say "a study by ___ suggests..." or "research shows that..." For my fellow nerds, I will direct you to giannabiscontini.com for these publications and more. For those of you who find citations distracting, you needn't worry about reading a book written by someone who has spent her lifetime immersed in the workings of human behavior. You will be free to float along, uninterrupted. And for those of you who sit in the middle, I have included some behavioral information in an appendix.

Now let's talk about this title.

A WORD ON THE F-WORD

Ladies, I swear like a tiny Italian sailor. It's a staple of my verbose existence.

When I moved to Southern California in 2012, I went full West Coast. I ramped up my yoga practice, drank more green juice, dropped my blood pressure, and spent more time outside. I became more peaceful in a big way. But one thing that never changed was my use of swear words to punctuate a point when necessary. While discussing and pitching this book, I heard each of the following:

"Do we really need so many F-words in this book?"

"Is the F-word truly necessary?"

"Can't you soften the title?"

"It will be more marketable if you don't swear."

"It won't sell with that word in the title."

I gave it thought. I even came up with ways to avoid swearing altogether. If used improperly, cursing can seem crass and classless. But if you *do* find that you are cringing or offended, ask yourself why. Is there possibly a belief that women should be quiet, demure, or proper? Is there a belief that only men can be smart, sophisticated, and kind *and* use the F-word…without judgment? Is there room to start challenging these beliefs even before diving fully into this book?

There is a bigger picture here: I realized that changing the title to be more appealing and make others comfortable, dimming down the fierceness to be more generically likable, would fly 100 percent in the face of the concept of this book. I was not about to accept the fuck that this guide for modern women would need to be soft to be appealing.

So you will see many F-words throughout this book, and I will do my best to honor its rightful place in our vocabulary. I find a well-placed F-word to be delightful. Lovely even. My wish for this book is for it to live fully in the world as intended, and I wish the same for you. Maybe this book sells a million copies; maybe only my mother buys it, but at least it will be out there being itself. Which is exactly the point.

Because here's the thing: fucks are *someone else's* stuff.

Fucks are not yours. They are someone else's fears, experiences, opinions, or thoughts. They might derail you completely, or maybe they're just a waste of time; they might serve someone else well but deplete you in the process. They might evoke martyrdom or earn you attention. They can be harmless or harmful. They almost always keep you liked.

But they are not true for *you*.

Fucks are the barriers to our favorite version of ourselves, the women we *bloom* into when we feel permission to live freely.

These could be endeavors we dedicate time to that we don't actually value or stories we sell ourselves ("I can't ____," "I'm not ____," "I should ____").

Fucks are dangerous because they look like they're true. They *sound* true. Everyone else behaves as though they *are* true. But even though we consciously, maybe even proudly, stay comfortably silent (Fuck #1) and live by these tired narratives, fucks don't really ever *feel* true.

In this book, we are going to explore the ten fucks I uncovered in my interviews, my observations, and my own experience:

1. Be Small
2. Be Soft
3. Be Less
4. Be the Exception
5. Be Stifled
6. Be Everything
7. Be Chosen
8. Be Dependent
9. Be Fixed
10. Be Sexy…but Sweet

By the end of this book, you will be completely free of *at least one* fuck. Exciting, I know. Think of it: one, giant, false story holding you back—*gone*.

You'll probably be tempted to go completely fuck-free all at once because it feels so darn good. But it's important that each false belief gets its deserved attention as you let it go. Why? Because change is hard. Life is busy, and we deserve to go easy on ourselves. There is also a great deal of emotion that may arise, as it did for me. These things take time, and you're worth it.

Living the *Fuckless* lifestyle means, in a word, liberation. It means designing and living your life on your terms. It's giving a knowing smile when someone gives you advice on what they would do, or what *you should do*, without really knowing who you are or what you want for yourself. It's truly enjoying the life you live instead of apologizing for it or feeling the guilt and shame that is projected at women who dare to live on their own terms. It might be having eight babies and moving to the suburbs to raise chickens. It might be choosing to remain single forever and giving a cheeky "I'm focused on other things," during the inevitable, "You're single…by choice?" conversations. It might be admitting that you want to trade in your dreams of a corner office for a life as an artist or vice versa.

No matter what you choose, there are some guarantees to this process:

- It will be uncomfortable.
- It will make others uncomfortable.
- It will challenge your status quo through new perspectives and behavior patterns.
- It will be one of the most freeing and satisfying experiences of your life.

In this guide, you will be supported through challenging your own false narratives so you can show up for yourself and more fully experience a life of your making. The life that you may not have even gotten the chance to realize you wanted. The life you constantly tell yourself is out of your reach.

For your benefit, I've divided this playbook into two parts:

1. **The Fucks You Were Given**: Learn about the ten fucks that derail you from who you are meant to be. Uncover where they came from, and choose which to drop in exchange for more freedom and fulfillment.
2. **Living (and Staying) Fuck-Free**: This is everything you need for letting go of the false beliefs of your choosing and then taking your *Fuckless*ness out into the world with strength, grace, and joy. Because this new lifestyle is too precious to lose.

This book was designed to help you challenge archaic systems and decide what, exactly, being female means to *you*. You will be asked to explore where your definition of female or feminine came from and consider whether it is ~~complete and utter trash~~ responsible for slowly crushing the soul of the majestic badass you know you are.

Even if you finish this book, throw it in the trash, and don't change a thing about your life, remember these three truths:

1. Your wants and needs are real and deserving of attention.
2. You will never truly benefit from denying your authentic self.
3. You are the only person responsible for your happiness.

There is really only one trick to this process: *be honest with yourself*. You didn't buy this book simply for inspiration, though I hope you are inspired. You didn't buy it because it's pretty, but of course my creative eye made sure it would look dope on your coffee table. You didn't buy it because you thought you could change your lifestyle via osmosis. The process of change and evolution is hard, but as long as you are honest with yourself, I promise that you will come out the other side better for having done it.

THE OTHER "F-WORD"

Female.

I strongly believe everyone holds some level of feminine energy within them. As I was writing this book, I discussed the concept with men, who shared their own frustrations on traditional gender narratives, how women are treated, and how they are "supposed" to act as men. While I didn't intend on interviewing males, I met many who asked if they could learn more about this book in order to better understand women and learn how to be better men. I included some of their stories as well, because it is necessary to approach this topic as a human issue and not a male vs. female endeavor. I appreciated their willingness to listen and not defend, to ask curious questions, and to consider alternative viewpoints. This gave me hope that we can all learn to listen, honor one another with respect, and refrain from judgment while being supported, not shamed, by the people around us. In addition to cisgender individuals, I also spoke with trans and nonbinary individuals who—you guessed it—also carry some fucks they're trying to drop.

This book, theoretically, is for anyone working to change their own narratives so they can live and breathe with more freedom and authenticity. However, I am well aware of my place in the world as a white cis female behavior scientist with privilege. And as a white cis female behavior scientist with privilege, I do my best not to discuss things I know nothing about. So while this book was born from my own experience and from what I have come to learn about how women are gendered and shaped in America, I hope it inspires many more books that include a closer look into the experiences of all genders, races, and cultures. That would be fascinating, and so needed.

To readers outside of the cis-female gender, I would be delighted to hear from you and learn more about your experiences. And I hope this book resonates with you and supports you in some way. Continuing this work takes all of us.

Dark Caves and Oh Shit Moments

When I was a kid, I went to summer camp near my home in the mountains of Pennsylvania. I was out in nature all day, and I loved it. One morning, we were on a hike and came across a cave. The counselors said they knew where the other end of the cave led to, but no one had ever made it all the way through because there was a small hole one had to crawl through in order to come out the other side. As the constant runt of the litter in every peer group I'd ever belonged to, I volunteered. My peers gasped. It was dangerous *and* it had never been done before. I felt brave, and I was hooked on the feeling of bravely entering the dark in order to reach the light.

That, and a particularly magnanimous girl offered me the brownie in her lunch.

The cave was one of the scariest places I'd ever been in my short life. The moment the light disappeared, I started imagining every creepy, terrifying thing around me. I imagined bats nesting in my hair, spiders crawling into my clothes, and my parents being informed of my tragic, albeit brave, death via a call from the counselors. Despite the fact that my mind was racing, I calmly felt around the cave walls until I made it to a very, *very* small hole. (It was several years until I learned the good swear words, but this would have been the moment to use one.) With my motivation to achieve hero status at the young age of seven, I began to try to squeeze myself through. I tried different ways to position my shoulders, then tried to go legs first, then considered giving up.

I wondered why no one told me exactly how small the freaking hole was. Weren't the counselors supposed to protect me from doing dumb shit like this? As I was fighting through, I was that determined kind of angry that makes you want to scream, cry, and take over the world all at once. I almost didn't make it. My arms burned as I pushed down on the rocks in order to shimmy my bottom through. I fell to the other side, covered in dirt and bugs, but I made it.

I could see the light.

I called out to my friends, allowing their voices to guide me the rest of the way. As I emerged, I triumphantly stood to receive cheers and accolades, imagining the story of the tiny hole-crawling explorer being told for centuries to come. On that day, I learned three lessons that would be reinforced in my life and in the lives of many others I would get to know over the next thirty-plus years:

- We never know what we're truly capable of until we face the thing we tell ourselves we can't do.
- Once we do, we realize we are exponentially braver and stronger than we ever imagined.
- The darkest caves hold the biggest lessons and the best stories.

If you're anything like me, easy stuff has always seemed aversive. It's boring. If I got hurt or failed while doing something easy, that wasn't noble. That wasn't an *adventure*. That was foolishness, carelessness, lame. Facing the dark caves of life, however—now there was something I was interested in. Maybe it's my East Coast upbringing. Maybe it's my crazy Italian genes screaming for the opportunity to be challenged in the face of adversity. Either way, I need more than one hand to count the number of times I've thought, *I could die like this. That's fine.* If jumping off a seventy-foot pole into a raging Laotian river was the end of me, at least it would be a great story.

Armed with this confidence, I was headed toward a life of bravery and adventure. Or so I thought.

I'm not certain when things started to change, but I know it began when I was very young and strengthened over time. I know it involved pain, disappointment, and harboring rare feelings of loneliness and unhappiness. I don't recall a particularly heavy situation that finally revealed to me what had occurred. It came on slowly. Painfully. Beautifully. Profoundly.

I was born wild, headstrong, and fearless. But over the course of the next three decades, my behavior began to follow *other* people's plans. My life was less and less something I took on with a knowing nobility and confidence. My needs and wants began to unfold according to what other people understood and rewarded. What other people expected. What other people felt comfortable with. I began to avoid doing anything that would cause friction or confusion for those around me. I found myself backing up and making sure my choices were okay with people who actually held no real jurisdiction in my life.

Every time we stay silent, take on someone else's work, let someone tell us we're not good enough, believe our needs and wants are undeserved, dismiss our natural feelings to keep someone else comfortable, believe we need someone else to be happy, or shame ourselves for our sex drive, body, or ambition, it's a little paper cut. It's making the choice to live on someone else's terms, over and over again, until we realize we have no idea who we are anymore.

The moment we realize we've lost ourselves feels like it comes on quickly, but it's cumulative. It's death by a thousand paper cuts. It's from *years* of accepting false beliefs about who we should be, even when we feel the incessant tugging from the truer, more fulfilling life that awaits us. It's self-harm. And that is no way to keep living our days.

There's a clarifying moment in many women's lives when we realize the repercussions of living according to how comfortable and happy it makes everyone else. We're exhausted. We've had enough. We want something else. We're slowly dying with our dreams still inside us.

And then there's the soul-crushing, earth-shattering moment

when we uncover that it's not *their* fault—not our partner, our parents, our kids, our boss, or our friends.

(Deep breath here.) It's *ours*.

Yeah. This is our very own, hopefully enlightening, definitely depressing Oh Shit Moment (OSM). The realization that we are responsible for most things in our lives—good, bad, and messy.

As you start this deep work, it's important to understand and accept that you are responsible for how you react to every thought, feeling, and action in your life. It is also critical that you understand it's not anyone else's job to give you what you want (this one was a bitch for me to learn). The sooner we can come to terms with this, the sooner we can stop wasting our time, boss up, and change the way we live.

Throughout the process of writing this book, I often imagined myself fiercely strutting around in an epic hair-flip-pointy-finger-hand-on-hip tirade, saying, "And as for *you*..." to anyone who has ever thrown you shade, derailed your dreams, or made you feel less than wonderful. Trust me, my head holds a whole other book on teaching people how to be less soul-crushing. But the purpose of this book isn't to regale you with my stories and those of others so we can sit in injustice or blame everyone else. It's to help you take a good look at your past, understand how you became who you became, and then set you off to change some things so you can live free from the need to be liked and "right" and from other people's opinions of who you should be. It isn't about changing everyone else, because that's impossible.

It's for you, about you.

If you've had your own OSM, it's a lot to take in. When we stop blaming the world around us and start looking inward, we make the brave choice to look past the roses and rainbows and see the parts we've been avoiding. The downside to this? It's a messy game. No one wants to see those parts of themselves, and society doesn't either. The upside? Once you get comfortable with the dark, your entire life changes. You receive lessons and experiences you wouldn't have received any other way.

While women have fought to advance and elevate themselves toward equitable treatment over the past century and change, many norms remain constant. Women are *still* conditioned to adapt to the expectations of others. To be the air and water that sustains—but does not disrupt—those around us.

To seek permission. To look to everyone else for answers. To give our power away. To stay small.

We bend, twist, and contort ourselves to serve the needs of others while triumphantly ignoring who *we* are meant to be, who we deeply know we are when we trust ourselves to live free from constant, if not subtle, judgment. We are careful to ensure happiness and comfort in those around us by avoiding confrontation, vulnerability, or anger. We silence our wild ideas, hide our ambitions, apologize for our overt strength, and even stifle our unbridled, insatiable sex drive.

We evolve to become our own worst critics, listening to the voices of those who've shaped us according to their *own* needs and ideas of what a woman should be. We become afraid of our own power and settle into a world of constant dissonance. A heartbreaking tug-of-war between who we are and who we are told we should be.

The glass ceiling is now a Glass *Box*. We incur judgment regardless of the direction in which we move.

We are conditioned over the course of our lives—not by one-off experiences but in a gradual environmental system that slowly signals to us what is acceptable and what is not. Many times, this is extremely helpful (e.g., learning to avoid adjusting your camel toe in public, learning to shake someone's hand firmly with eye contact when you meet them), but beyond the basics, this system is *broken*. It's constructed of old, tired narratives and in great need of recalibration. And when you realize how broken it is, it's horrifying. It's also life-changing.

Because we are heavily influenced by what we are told and how we are treated, we have reinforced the same stories about ourselves, and females in general, for years or even decades.

Until we change our perspectives and understand exactly how we have become the women we are today, we will continue to look in all the wrong places as we try to find fulfillment in tomorrow.

Decade after decade, women relentlessly receive the message— through politics, fashion magazines, formal education, society, social media, entertainment, and even our own circles—that we are wrong, weak, too much, too little, emotionally inconvenient, intellectually inferior, or otherwise something to be fixed. We receive confusing messages about our behavior in contrast with the male gender. What is "passion" in men is traditionally considered "emotional" for women. The trait of "leadership" in a man is reduced to "bossy" or, for those with simpler vocabularies, "bitchy" if you happen to possess a vagina. Whereas men are encouraged to become multidimensional, independent, and *interesting* individuals, the world is supremely confused by (and concerned for) a woman with a dozen hobbies and no partner.

Women, be *liked*. Men, be *anything*.

I believe you are more. More than the expectations set upon you. More than the judgment that raised you or, more accurately, held you down, ensuring you stayed quietly seated. More than the Glass Box in which you've been living, skillfully maneuvering in ways that avoid intimidating, challenging, or upsetting others.

I know you, and you're over it.

Maybe you perceive the world through the lens of opportunity and feel the rush of adrenaline when faced with a challenge. Maybe you're a happily single woman who enjoys igniting flirtation at the bat of an eyelash, or maybe you've decided not to have a partner at all. Maybe you have aspirations beyond the traditional—beyond what is familiar and comfortable—like traveling the world or starting a business. Maybe you don't know *what* you want yet, but you know it's not the life you get up and live every day. And that's okay too.

You will soon learn how to embrace the luxury of not giving a fuck what anyone else thinks. You will be free from the constant, exhausting, stressful juggling that functions to keep you liked and acceptable at all times.

The time to be your wild, beautiful self is literally now. Because if not now, *when*?

Saddle up. You're on your way to finally being *Fuckless*.

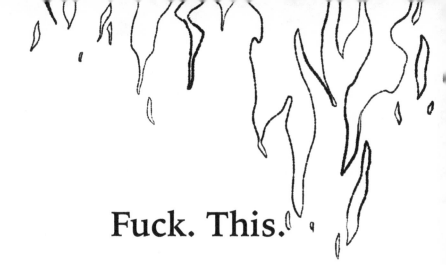

Fuck. This.

It was a gorgeous June day in 2019.

I was driving a rented VW Beetle to Napa for the weekend. My windows were down, and the music was up.

That weekend, I would volunteer at the Huichica Music Festival and spend time with my husband in the Calistoga house a family friend gave us the keys to years ago. On the way, I took a promising investment meeting with a well-known businessman in my industry while driving the majestic cliffside roads of Stinson Beach. I pulled over and found my way to an overlook, falling into a trance with the typical California scene. Roadtrippers and nature lovers wandered paths without agenda. When I called my father to share my gratitude and happiness, he said that he loved me and was proud of me.

I wove my way up the coast, the blue Pacific beckoning me to steal glances. I thought about my perfect Santa Ynez wedding and devoted husband, my world travel, my blooming company, the book I was writing with a dear friend and colleague, and my incredibly close relationships with friends and family.

I had created and manifested this life.

I felt rooted. I was living how I had always wanted to live.

I was deeply, wholly happy.

I rode this high for a full month, until July 7.

It was the day the U.S. Women's National Soccer team fought for the World Cup in a match against the Netherlands. I'd been religiously watching the games and looking forward to this day for weeks. I loved watching badass women conquer their sport.

The game was energizing in a way I'd never experienced. Each time Megan Rapinoe threw her arms up in her famous stance, I gained more energy. I watched the US earn their medals and rock their victory for weeks afterward. They were celebrated everywhere they went, and they didn't apologize for it or feign the demure tone expected of women. They not only celebrated their own success, but they also used their platform to fight for equal pay and inspire women everywhere. These women were the role models I never had. In fact, they were the role models I wanted to be. I was fired up and living into the fullest expression of my power to date. I hadn't ever felt anything like this power before, but I *liked* it.

I also felt naive and a little stupid. I was thirty-seven. I had a handful of master's degrees. I owned a gorgeous California craftsman home. I was building my own company. I had a great husband. My voice and ideas had been broadcast in over one hundred countries. I had been interviewed for magazines and dubbed a pioneer and thought leader in my field. *I* was one people looked up to.

So what did I need a role model for?

I realized that throughout my life, many people were happy to give me well-intended advice on where to go to school, how to run my business, who to date, and what not to eat, wear, think, or say. However, zero people had guided me on simply being myself. There was always something else I should or could have been doing to fit in with expectations. And I needed to see women doing it differently.

That day cracked open something I'd been hiding from myself: the feeling of what it would be like to live my life *in full*. Out loud. Unapologetically and on my own terms. It was also the first day of the last two months of my marriage, which became the catalyst for the following two years of trauma, illness, growth, and change.

The day before the game, I went out with my husband. It was a perfect San Diego morning, and we were enjoying brunch (and brunch drinks) with friends. We had agreed to go home afterward, and we did. But I could see the bar beckoning him back. We discussed the role of alcohol in our relationship—*again*—and I ended up back at the bar with him until one in the morning—*again*—because staying silent and following his instruction to "just be happy" was what I had learned to do to be a good, fun wife.

I woke up in the morning hungover. Again. But for the first time, I was *enraged*. While I lay there, head and heart pounding, I thought back over my pleas to go home, to reduce our alcohol intake, and to start waking up early to enjoy morning bike rides like we used to.

Then it hit me. The one person I had trusted to care about my health and well-being didn't. And I had allowed it.

When the US team won the World Cup just a few hours later, it sealed my fate as a woman who was done living against what she knew she wanted for herself. Done with "good enough." Done with staying small. Done with plastering a smile on my face. Done with waking up every day feeling like I had to "just be happy" and that I should stop wanting more for myself. Done going without the deep conversations and frequent travel promised to me in his vows. Done fighting to be taken seriously. Done working with people who promised me things but never delivered. Done pretending my feelings weren't hurt. Done dumbing down my vocabulary and ambition and bank account. Done swallowing everything and feeling like nothing.

I was just *done giving a fuck.*

By the time I finally began to unapologetically take agency over my own life, I felt I had waited too long (as most of us do). And by the time I got to any point of real change, I'd spent three decades making decisions about my life based on other people's opinions, fears, and needs.

While I had been busy unknowingly giving everyone else jurisdiction over my future, I made the same mistakes over and over *and over.* It would ultimately cost me six figures, my marriage, my self-worth, and almost my life.

During this time, which I affectionately refer to as "the emotional coup on my soul," I looked back on an entire life of chasing validation—other people's thoughts and feelings about what a female looked like and acted like and how she lived her life.

I am of the strong belief that sometimes you have to break down to break through, and that is exactly what happened in the ensuing months as my eyes began to open.

The book project I spent two years leading ended in an infuriating battle of ethics and gaslighting from my male counterparts. I realized that the same dear friends and businessmen who'd made promises to invest in my company had stolen proprietary information and my business plan and had used me for the name and brand I'd built. These notoriously predatory individuals groomed me to believe I needed them in order to run my own company. While these "venture capitalists" obtained my trust and sent the message that I needed them (Fuck #3), I put confidence in them because I lacked it in myself.

I would soon be divorced. My marriage was good enough, but I struggled with the feeling that I was losing who I was and what I wanted in a sea of alcohol and lip service. And after years of swallowing my wants and needs (Fucks #1, #5, and #7), an unexpected betrayal made it easier for me to choose myself.

My father was months from severe dementia and neurological decline (he eventually passed away a year after the day I decided to leave my marriage—two weeks before the pandemic restrictions lifted and I had plans to see him). As he fell further into his illness, he often cried to me about his behavior as a father.

It tore open wounds I had bandaged as a child, and they were so much more jolting in the light of my mid-thirties. I realized that I grew up believing that men naturally hurt women because they just don't know any better (Fuck #5). I also saw how I learned to excuse and downplay their behavior while giving as much of my emotional labor as I could muster in the name of supporting them (Fuck #6).

When I raised concerns with my business partner about her lack of work ethic and her inability to produce results, she became enraged and entitled: yelling, crying, and spinning out of control. Before I could reconvene for a more productive discussion, she started what would become thirteen months of litigation for every piece of the company I had designed, built, and grown.

I became entangled with a man internationally famous for his inspiring talks on leadership and being a good human, only to be gaslighted and physically taken advantage of in the darkest relationship of my life. Months later, I discovered his business partner's ties to Harvey Weinstein and Jeffrey Epstein.

I landed in the emergency room, my stomach bleeding from stress and trauma.

My beloved rescue pup I adopted during the pandemic was diagnosed with a neurological disorder, requiring more vigilance, care, and love than I thought I was prepared to give. Six months later, my other rescue was diagnosed with cancer.

After my father's celebration of life event (which I planned and hosted in my hometown six months after his death), my mother turned cold and sharp. We got into an argument that rocked my world as I saw even more of how much she was affected by the same gendering I had experienced.

A friend's son with special needs tragically passed away.

My cousin, who had suffered from mental illness for over a decade, committed suicide.

My scale read ninety-two pounds.

I spent two years of holidays alone.

I was now solely financially responsible for my mortgage and not able to work.

This shitstorm of upheaval rocked my world. Something or someone seriously wanted to make sure I was paying attention. It was all too much, too fast. In the midst of it, I forced a smile in conversations with friends, hanging on by a thread while listening to their wedding plans, career successes, and pregnancy news. Their lives were blossoming while mine was falling apart. One night, I went to dinner with a friend. She told me about her successful company, amazing husband, and plans for a baby.

Driving home, I very seriously considered ending my life.

I vividly remember walking into my house and over to my kitchen drawer. As I opened it, calmly and with purpose, I noticed that my Japanese knife was missing. I was jarred back into reality and shocked at the thoughts in my head that said, very clearly, *I do not want to do this anymore.* I slowly turned around, walked over to my couch, and tried to breathe deeply.

I told myself, *Just stay here. Don't move. All you have to do is sit right here and breathe.*

If you had told me that it would all start to unravel just one month from that gorgeous, happy weekend in Napa, I would've called you crazy.

That dark time took me down. It nearly took me out. But through tears, naps on my kitchen floor, and the total life upheaval I couldn't control, I got to thinking about some things. Mostly, how I got there.

After I realized the strength of my compulsion to avoid my unsettled past (and present) by throwing myself into work, I knew it was my cue to keep pulling the thread of whatever lesson was being forced upon me. To stay seated in whatever was happening.

The uncomfortable got more uncomfortable.

I stayed seated.

It became unbearable.

I stayed seated.

That's when I realized I was choosing to lie in a bed of my own making. This was possibly the hardest part of it all.

Then I cried. And cried. And cried.

This complete stop was not peaceful. I was not the woman sitting in her beautiful home on her expensive meditation pillow, calmly taking a few moments to center herself.

I. Was. *Tragic.*

I felt ridiculous, but something within me felt like I had to show people this side. I spent the next few weeks allowing myself to suffer out loud. In front of people. I think it was my way of being unapologetic, saying, "This is okay. This is where I am right now. I need this." I tried to normalize it because honestly, it *is* normal. As a society, we don't treat reevaluating our lives and deeply, unabashedly exploring our wants and needs as normal or healthy, because it's awkward as hell. Years of strong cocktails and toxic positivity are just so much easier. Talking about how things are *going* to change or how *we're going to get our shit together*, but never really knowing how to make those moves, is easier. More acceptable. Less emotional and off-putting.

As I began to get honest with myself, I thought about my past. I thought about being bullied as a kid. I thought about how I entered survival mode and became a bully myself. I thought about my father taking pictures of me in my bathing suit and printing them out so he could more effectively point out parts of my thirteen-year-old body that were unacceptable. I thought about how no matter what my father did, my mother would comfort me by saying, "Oh, honey, he's just being a man." I thought about how that ridiculous justification is never applied to women, who seem to be expected to learn from their mistakes and grow to be better.

I looked back on twenty years of romantic relationships, realizing I had yet to "meet my match" because I was taught that an empathetic, thoughtful, emotionally and intellectually secure man (i.e., a good match) was not something I could expect. In fact, until I was well into my thirties, I accepted that my passion and intellect were something that had to be dumbed down if I ever wanted to have a partner at all (Fuck #8).

I thought about how many men had told me how brilliant I was but looked at me as if I was lost when I pulled up a seat at their table. I thought about the fact that "strength" is primarily seen as aggressive and masculine and needs a serious rebranding in order to save the health of our society. I thought about whether I wanted to continue giving most of my life to my company. I thought about how my self-worth was based on my physical appearance (Fuck #10), and how I spoke to myself about my own body. And how, when I finally learned to accept and love my body, I berated myself for not achieving at twenty-five what most would expect of a successful forty-year-old.

Because I was conditioned to always feel shame for *something*.

I thought about how I spoke to myself about everything. For the first time, I thought about how *those voices were not mine*. I realized that my whole life was, in fact, not mine. And my body, mind, and soul had finally had enough.

I lost my ability to envision where I wanted to go in life, something I easily did most mornings during my meditation. One day I woke up and couldn't move my neck. I developed an eye twitch, headaches, and hives. Every little thing felt like it would push me into an ugly cry. Most days, toward the end, it did. Emotionally, physically, and mentally, I was just done. Everything felt out of control. And I couldn't do anything about it.

These tears were not the soundtrack of a well-deserved pity party or a freeing catharsis. They were the result of my expertise as a darn good behavior analyst. As much as I longed to place blame and defer responsibility for not becoming the full expression of the woman I wanted to be (yet), I knew that behavior is bidirectional. I knew that, while the limiting, running narrative in my head was composed of voices that weren't mine, I had allowed my behavior to follow.

I allowed everyone else's desires and opinions to be a copout for running my own life.

Building a life based on everyone else—and, as a result, believing that who *I* wanted to be was wrong—was easier than making my own decisions. I became a master at allowing other people's fucks to sit squarely on my shoulders because doing so gave me an excuse not to shine, or worse, to fail.

It was easier. But it wasn't better. I realized I wasn't ever happier or more fulfilled by taking the easy way. Some people are, and there's nothing wrong with that. It just wasn't me. And it's probably not you either. This led me to ask a very simple question that changed my life:

What if I just stopped giving so many fucks?

I contemplated this question as I sat in the bathtub of my LA apartment, on the top floor of a Tudor mansion I'd treated myself to while escaping a former life. No one thing had pushed me to this place; *everything* had pushed me to this place. I was sobbing, doubled over in a combination of emotional pain and anger, breaking into pieces. *Again.*

But for the first time, with that curious question tugging at my heart, I was clear.

Because so much in my life had been taken away and disrupted, I was filled with a strong gratitude for what remained. It made me fiercely protective of my own happiness and what was left of my life. I wanted to rise, if only to show others it was possible. I realized there was no other answer than to break free from everything I thought I knew about how to live as a woman in the world and change the way I did *everything*.

I felt I had no choice but to do something desperate and big. I reevaluated my life from a completely honest perspective. I saw the messy stuff I was hiding from. I got real and angry, which led to freedom and joy. I peeled the layers off of gendered narratives and changed the way I made decisions. I spent more time with people who energized me and gently created space from those who depleted me. I began to trust myself without judgment or hesitation, as I naturally had as a child. I moved my life to a small bayside town, got healthy in every sense of the word, pivoted my career, and spent more time writing books and learning about subjects that ignited me. And so much more. With nothing to lose and fueled with curiosity as to what I would gain, I started my social experiment.

I became *Fuckless*.

Part One

The Fucks
We're Given

A healthy dose of energy, passion, and inspiration can carry us through big changes. Think of this section as an educational caffeine shot for the soul.

In this larger, meatier section, we take a serious, cutthroat look at the fucks you've been given by well-intended loved ones, social media, society, politics, and general commercialism. This will aid you in sending new signals for who you are and what you want from the world.

Be Small

fuck #1

"What struck me—with her and with many other female American friends I have—is how invested they are in being "liked." How they have been raised to believe that their being likable is very important and that this "likable" trait is a specific thing. And that specific thing does not include showing anger or being aggressive or disagreeing too loudly."

—CHIMAMANDA NGOZI ADICHIE,
WE SHOULD ALL BE FEMINISTS

This fuck is a big one.

The notion that being female means being vocally and physically small, thus remaining likable and approachable, is likely the *biggest*, most dangerous, most BS fuck of all. Unfortunately, this belief still holds strong in the archaic rulebook that guides the expectations of females today. Thoughtfully challenging this message by understanding where it came from and how our own avoidance contributes to this message can change the world.

"Shrinking Women," a poem written by Lily Myers and performed at Wesleyan University's 2013 College Unions Poetry Slam Invitational rocked my world. Our behavior is shaped by our environments, and if you grew up as Lily Myers did—as many of us did—then these scenes played a part in why you may believe being a woman means being physically and vocally small.

I've included the poem here to help prepare us to dive into this concept. It is also available online, and it is powerful.

> *Across from me at the kitchen table, my mother smiles*
> *over red wine that she drinks out of a measuring glass.*
> *She says she doesn't deprive herself,*
> *but I've learned to find nuance in every*
> *movement of her fork.*
> *In every crinkle in her brow as she offers me*
> *the uneaten pieces on her plate.*
> *I've realized she only eats dinner when I suggest it.*
> *I wonder what she does when I'm not there to do so.*
>
> *Maybe this is why my house feels bigger each*
> *time I return; it's proportional.*
> *As she shrinks the space around her seems increasingly vast.*
> *She wanes while my father waxes. His stomach has grown*
> *round with wine, late nights, oysters, poetry. A new*
> *girlfriend who was overweight as a teenager, but*
> *my dad reports that now she's "crazy about fruit."*
>
> *It was the same with his parents;*
> *as my grandmother became frail and angular her husband*
> *swelled to red round cheeks, round stomach*
> *and I wonder if my lineage is one of women shrinking*

making space for the entrance of men into their lives
not knowing how to fill it back up once they leave.

I have been taught accommodation.
My brother never thinks before he speaks.
I have been taught to filter.
"How can anyone have a relationship to food?"
 He asks, laughing, as I eat the black bean
 soup I chose for its lack of carbs.
I want to tell say: we come from difference, Jonas,
you have been taught to grow out
I have been taught to grow in
you learned from our father how to emit, how to
 produce, to roll each thought off your tongue
 with confidence, you used to lose your voice
 every other week from shouting so much
I learned to absorb
I took lessons from our mother in
 creating space around myself
I learned to read the knots in her forehead
 while the guys went out for oysters
and I never meant to replicate her, but
spend enough time sitting across from someone
 and you pick up their habits

that's why women in my family have
 been shrinking for decades.
We all learned it from each other, the way each
 generation taught the next how to knit
weaving silence in between the threads
which I can still feel as I walk through
 this ever-growing house,

skin itching,
picking up all the habits my mother has unwittingly
   dropped like bits of crumpled paper from
   her pocket on her countless trips from
   bedroom to kitchen to bedroom again,
Nights I hear her creep down to eat plain yogurt
   in the dark, a fugitive stealing calories
   to which she does not feel entitled.
Deciding how many bites is too many
How much space she deserves to occupy.

Watching the struggle I either mimic or hate her,
And I don't want to do either anymore
but the burden of this house has followed
   me across the country
I asked five questions in genetics class today and
   all of them started with the word "sorry."
I don't know the requirements for the sociology major
   because I spent the entire meeting deciding whether
   or not I could have another piece of pizza
a circular obsession I never wanted but

inheritance is accidental
still staring at me with wine-stained lips
   from across the kitchen table.

Mic drop.

In every sense of the word, women typically hear undertones
of "be small" throughout our lives. I am horrified to say that as
young as seven or eight, my parents' friends would compliment

me by saying things like, "You're so pretty and petite!" and never, "You've gone nine straight semesters on the honor roll!"

As if that wasn't enough to mold my understanding of what was acceptable and where my worth was to be found and cultivated, these compliments included helpful follow-up warnings like, "Petite girls can get rounder as they grow older," or "Be careful you don't start growing *out* as you grow *up!*" While I grew up a ballet dancer, I never actually remember anyone discussing anyone's weight when I was in the studio. It probably occurred, but I likely brushed it off as a part of the dancing culture. However, my parents' friends were "real" people in the "real" world. I absolutely saw my ballet life as separate from "real" life; growing up with heroine-chic, chain-smoking Russians who drank vodka for breakfast while a man in nerd glasses played piano in the studio corner was not anywhere near reality. But if "real" adults were giving me these warnings, they must be true. My parents looked on proudly while the internal narrative built in my head, still invisible to everyone in the room.

When I was thirteen, I was walking through the yard to our pool. Unbeknownst to me at the time, my father, who was taking pictures of his garden, turned his camera on me. A few days later, he showed me the pictures and made comments about the parts of my ninety-pound body that were unacceptable for a bikini. He did this in a tone that sounded kind and helpful. While I felt humiliated and angry, I also digested this as normal. I learned, as we all do, "You are not okay. Be smaller." This fuck was reinforced when I observed my father publicly refer to my mother as "fat-ass" around their friends. I know of several women who saw this, became enraged, and said nothing.

My father continued for years to make nonsexual but very uncomfortable comments about women's bodies and genuinely did not understand why it was inappropriate. Many men his age didn't either. One day, he and I were walking into his warehouse when one of his employees said, "Your girlfriends are getting younger and younger, Richard!" as if it were to be taken as a casual joke and not the most disgusting thing ever to be said in front of a teenager.

NOTE

At points in this book, it might sound as if I've had a "tough" family life. I feel that "tough" is a relative term and that no one can judge anyone else's circumstances. However, I was raised as a white, privileged female with a trust fund and a private school education. My parents and I have been on great terms for a long time. This is my point. These situations do not only occur for those with deadbeat parents or terrible friends. My father, who I miss every day, was my biggest cheerleader and the single most positively influential person in my life. He taught me to love nature, invest in my well-being and education, and listen and help others wherever I could, and he inspired me to travel the world. This is a very real example of how someone who loves you very much can still pass along the shitty beliefs they were given.

About a year before starting this book, I was watching a documentary on war crimes and terrorism. A terrorist being interviewed stated that one of the strategies used by corrupt governments came in a message they received firsthand: "Take out the women." He explained that those who intended to corrupt a territory knew that if they could silence the women, the oppression would sustain. The women were the ones making noise, rebelling, consistent in their efforts to disrupt their plans.

From loved ones to terrorists, when women are silenced, it affects entire societies, laws, and even climate change.

Where would the women's movement be without organizations like 9to5 or #MeToo? Without women like Gloria Steinem, Jane Fonda, the late Ruth Bader Ginsberg, Geena Davis, or Betty Friedan? Where would education and climate change be without the uproarious passion of two of my favorite *Fuckless* females, Malala Yousafzai and Greta Thunberg? How fucking boring would that World Cup win have been if each player had just politely smiled, curtsied, and gone home with her medal instead of soaking the locker room with champagne and then continuing to light the world of gender-based pay inequality on fire?

None of those women give a fuck (anymore), and it's changing the world.

* * *

Let's take a look at a simplification of every interaction we have. This is generally how we learn much of our behavior in social scenarios, whether it is to be silent, dress a certain way, or keep taking shit from the boss:

- **Antecedent**: Someone does something.
- **Behavior**: You react.
- **Consequence**: Their behavior is reinforced or punished

(more or less likely to happen in the future under similar conditions).

In action, it looks something like this scenario I witnessed recently:

- **Antecedent**: A colleague makes a comment about a coworker's attitude as it relates to her menstrual cycle (charming).
- **Behavior**: You smile awkwardly and leave the room, mentally throat-punching said colleague. Some other colleagues remain in the room to snicker and laugh.
- **Consequence**: The colleague who made the comment feels like the epitome of cool because they made people laugh.

What happened there?

The individual with the clever menstruation joke is reinforced (i.e., likely to make similar jokes again with the people who laughed), and you feel a little bit defeated and/or angry, which is justified.

You avoided having to deal with it, which I get. We only have so much energy. But you have also taught them that you, and maybe others, will tolerate similar behavior in the future. As someone who analyzes behavior for a living, I understand the immense power of consequences for behaviors—in this case, staying silent. Research estimates that consequences are responsible for at least 80 percent of future behavior. So, in our quest to be liked, we make ourselves silent and small, but others (and their actions) continue to grow tall.

Avoidance is powerful. If we are successful in avoiding an uncomfortable reaction as a result of speaking up (and this is at work, at home, and in life), our avoidant behavior is rewarded. This is called negative reinforcement (more on that in the appendix). We avoided awkwardness, judgment, or worse, and we are likely to continue to do so. But does it change anything for you or for women in general? Leaving the room, remaining silent, or speaking up to someone uninvolved isn't strong enough to create change. It gives you something to do, but it doesn't *get* you anywhere. You can bet on that irritating comment or downright shocking thing happening again. In the meantime, you learn to act out of fear and avoidance; it works for you. You learn to be silent. Worse, you teach *others* that you're silent.

From there, it's another joke, then a microaggression, then maybe an inappropriate touch. Obviously, not every male who makes unprofessional jokes is capable of or likely to sexually harass or assault someone. However, this is how the waters get tested. It's a process of seeing how much someone will tolerate and what the possible consequences for the jokester's future behavior might be. It is also an opportunity to shame someone for not appreciating the joke, letting her know that she will receive the same punishment in the future if she speaks up, so she has to make the choice between being liked and speaking her mind.

Then where is the line?

Wherever you draw it.

Life is a series of moments that ask us to weigh reward and punishment according to our own needs and wants.

You might be thinking, *I deal with that kind of thing all the time.*

It's not worth it to say anything. That's fair. But consider this: what do you mean by "it's not worth it"? What do you think will happen in return if you drop a sarcastic, "Cool joke, Brad"?

You'll be called a name? You'll look like the fun police? They'll say something mean about you? It'll be an awkward moment?

That's Fuck #1 looking you straight in the face.

Be nice. Be quiet. You might make them feel bad. They won't like you. Don't say anything or you'll look (insert pejorative fuck-based adjective here).

Consider the times you felt the need to speak up or stand tall; is it a *you* problem or a *them* problem? Are you simply wanting to do your best or maybe speak up against an injustice? Do you speak up less frequently or take up less space because of fears of being on the receiving end of a woman who chooses *not* to be small?

A woman who is thought of as:

- shrill
- a show-off
- bossy
- a pain in the ass

When we buy into this fuck and allow it to control us, a situation that may have benefited from our voice, opinion, skills, or solution never sees the light of day, all because we give our power away and stay small. Why? Many times it's for the same reason we adhere to the fucks explored in the rest of this book.

We are taught to value being liked over being loud, talented, powerful, or nearly anything else we may want for ourselves.

This is called *positive reinforcement contingent upon social attention*, and it's very, very strong (also in the appendix).

Sure, people of all genders generally want to be liked, but the difference here is in our learning. Men do not typically receive the message that their value lies in how much they are liked or approved of. In fact, we tend to further empower and reward men who rock the boat, disrupt, and maybe piss people off along the way (because that's what happens when you're crushing life). Women are not generally encouraged to be boisterous or headstrong or to challenge the status quo without a double dose of hurtful, punishing, oppressive insults (also known as punishment if it decreases the likelihood of that behavior in the future). This allows us to be kept quietly under control.

But what if we decided to say, "Fuck it"?

What might a world filled with loud, unapologetic women like our World Cup team be like? Really fucking fun, right?

Here's how the choice to stay small strengthens societal gender stereotypes:

Person A is conditioned to be brave, outspoken, and confident. They grow up rarely questioning themselves, so the world does not question them either. Their behavior is reinforced. They may gain jobs based on confidence, not competence, and they may end up having trouble being questioned. The world is in orbit around them, and they have power. They fail to acknowledge or consider other people's desires, fears, and needs because they have not been expected to. Or maybe they have not been approached in an effective way to modify this behavior, or consequences have never been strong enough to warrant change.

Person B is conditioned to be small, wait their turn, question themselves, and/or defer to others. As they grow up, they meet many like Person A, who reinforce this belief and silence them, treat them as if they are less valuable, second-guess them, and otherwise put them behind the mark.

Person B learns that while they *feel* this treatment is unjust, the world does not share this belief. Person B's attempts to speak up, take up space, earn a job they've worked hard for, and enter into relationships where they are treated equally are punished. Now Person B really *is* small, hesitant, and likely to orbit around Person A, waiting for permission.

Person A sees this and feels their dominant role is justified, because "that's just how things are."

I've listened to many women complain about the men in their workplace. And I get it. Some are easy to complain about. To be fair, so is everyone. These women speak of boys' clubs, sexist comments, and shocking behavior; this has never been more prevalent than in today's post-Trump climate, and I'm thankful it's all getting out into the open for further observation and discussion.

I listen to their frustration and anger and say, "Ugh, awful. So then what did you do?"

"I just left the room."

"I didn't say anything."

"I called you to vent about it."

Here's where the "yeah, buts" come in.

I say, "What do you think about coming up with something to say next time so you don't feel so small and silent?"

"Yeah, but I'll get in trouble." (For *what*?)

"Yeah, but I didn't want to seem emotional." (See Fuck #5.)

"Yeah, but I guess it wasn't bad enough to say anything." (You sure? Sounds pretty uncomfortable.)

"Yeah, but that's not going to change anything, so what's the point?" (You don't know that.)

"Yeah, but I'm too nice to say anything." (You are not being nice. You are afraid of speaking up—maybe rightly so. But I doubt anyone has ever told you, "You are *so* nice! You never stand up against injustices or for your own beliefs, and you always let others shine in their ignorance and hurtful comments!")

The minute you stay small, you participate in writing a blank check for someone else's behavior and essentially sign up to tolerate the same scenario again. By staying silent, you are at that very moment choosing to live on someone else's terms, and you reinforce their thinking—that you are small, on the sidelines, insignificant. It doesn't feel good. It's disempowering. Avoiding the awkwardness, courage, and skill required to speak up according to what you value is never going to give you the tools to become better, stronger, or more powerful. It's never going to give the other person an opportunity to learn, and it's never going to evolve the way people behave as a society.

So why do we do it? Why do we stay vocally and physically small? Punishment in the form of name calling, eye rolls, snickers, intimidation, side glances, exasperated sighs, body shaming, and being told that our response to an injustice is wrong, bothersome, or an overreaction. We are made to feel disliked or wrong for speaking up, for standing tall and talented, and we somehow believe it.

While you're considering whether you would benefit from dropping this fuck, also consider what it would mean for you to be tall. To have an opinion and share it. To learn the ninja communication skills to respectfully get your point across and come out looking like a model of grace and power. To build a way of living that says, unapologetically, "I'm being tall today, and I'm sincerely unaffected by how that makes you feel." Or, "I am not the problem; your hurtful comments are, and it's cool if you're mad at me for speaking up about it."

By now I'm sure you can tell this isn't just about some clown making period jokes. This is about the power you have as a woman and understanding that:

- It threatens people who are afraid of being recognized as small themselves.
- Those people's opinions are none of your business.
- Anyone who wants you to stay small is holding you back with a fuck you don't need.

- If you want to be taller and louder, it's on you.

No one ever said it was easy, but I can tell you it's worth it. I own this particular belief. I don't apologize for it, and I've learned to live loudly without also being an asshole. Most of the time.

Adhering to the idea that women should be small and therefore likable gets us exactly nowhere. When I dropped this fuck, six (yes, really, *six*) things happened:

1. I garnered more respect from others (even though I didn't necessarily aim for that).
2. I made more money.
3. I found myself surrounded by great people who would do anything to support me.
4. I found it easier to identify and avoid individuals who serve their ego by holding others down.
5. I increased relationships with like-purposed people.
6. I became happier, lighter, and more energized.

That feels strange and commercialized to look at in print. *Do this! You'll become a millionaire and meet the partner of your dreams!* False. You know better than to latch on to that story and expect life to turn into rainbows and unicorns. However, those six things are very much true for me, and I challenge you to try dropping this fuck of all fucks to see what will change for you.

Don't play small. Don't stay silent. Silence isn't golden; it's darkness.

I do not shrink.
I shine.

Fuck
Being Small

Consider with curiosity:

- When and with whom is being small rewarded?
- When and with whom is taking up space, speaking your mind, and bringing your A-game rewarded?
- Where did this story of small and silent come from?
- What is maintaining it, and what are you getting from it?
- What is likely to happen if you keep this fuck?

YOUR REWRITE

In the following exercise, fill in the blanks when you feel inspired and clear. You can choose to commit to these new beliefs any time you're ready.

1. I'm dropping the belief that

....

....

2. Because

....

....

3. If I'm successful, (what will happen?)

....

....

4. If I'm successful, I will have time and energy for

....

....

5. And it will feel

....

....

6. My new belief is

....

....

7. And I will show this by (be specific: actions, words, phrases, etc.)

....

....

Be Soft

"For me, being a girl...being a woman...was the end. If you wanted to live and you wanted to have power and you wanted to succeed, you were a boy. Most girls, man, we're feisty when we're young, before puberty sets in. And it's when the specter of womanhood begins to loom on the horizon that you have to stuff anger, you have to be a 'good girl.'"

—ACTOR AND ACTIVIST JANE FONDA IN THE DOCUMENTARY *FEMINISTS: WHAT WERE THEY THINKING?*

In addition to the belief that women should be small, we continue to tell young girls and women to be soft, avoiding any kind of moves that signal power, control, or dominance. They learn the following about strength:

- It is a male characteristic.
- Females who demonstrate this trait are off-putting or aggressive.
- It involves coercion, force, a loud voice, or a harsh demeanor.

However, our current idea of strength no longer fits modern society; it actually results in the opposite of the followership it was formerly designed to elicit. So let's talk about being soft and strong, what we're conditioned to believe, and where we might want to think about heading as a species.

Studies on primates show that being an alpha male (i.e., "strong") isn't all it's cracked up to be.

Duke anthropologist Brian Hare and his wife, Vanessa, a science writer, studied why cooperation and compromise may bust the myth that dominant, strong alpha males are the most successful. An NPR article by Bret Stetka reviewed their work and makes an interesting—and for humans, maybe a predictive—point:

> Violence and aggression…wasn't always a sound evolutionary strategy. Being the alpha bully means you're more often engaged in dangerous encounters, and a target of the greater group, in whose best interest it is to weed out threatening, socially destabilizing males.
>
> "When you look back in nature and see when a species or group of species underwent a major transition or succeeded in a new way, friendliness, or an increase in cooperation, are typically part of that story," says Hare.

Species experiencing a major transition start to weed out the bullies, you say…

This is showing what we are already seeing in post-pandemic life. When strength shows up in its traditional masculine form, it is more likely to piss people off than to gain sustainable followers or a romantic partner.

And gorillas aren't the only ones beating their chests as a sign they rule the roost.

A certain kind of woman was accepted into the boys' club, and that woman was me. I learned to drink bourbon, make fun of the guys, and work hard, but I also learned to never harbor the delusion that I was as good or as powerful as they were.

In an organization in which I held a high title, I once made a joke about one of the executives that resulted in an uproar of laughter. As if it were a knee-jerk reaction, he bent me over, put my head in between his legs, and spanked me. He laughed while carrying out the act, as if it were the same kind of joke. It wasn't, and everyone knew it. The room, filled only with men, fell silent. My face flushed red with embarrassment, and I had a rare moment where I felt like I wanted to burst into tears. He backpedaled, as most do, trying to play it off as funny. But it wasn't funny. It was an assertion of dominance from someone who couldn't handle feeling like anything other than the untouchable force in the room.

It was also a warning, and I took it as such: *I am the strong one here. Do not cross me.* Later, in a private moment, he apologized and dismissed his behavior as a "wolf pack" moment. Whatever that meant. I looked him straight in the eyes and said, while fighting back tears, "Don't you ever, *ever* touch me again."

As you can tell, this fuck is complex and cloudy because by very definition we are misusing the words "strong" and "soft." We have it so incredibly backward. Not only do we tell women to be soft—which, to me, appears to mean taking other people's shit with a smile—but we tell men that masculine means anything *but* soft. Even "soft skills" are seen as less important (we talk about them like they're critical, and they are, but when is the last time you put "empathetic" on a resume? Ever been promoted solely because of your positive attitude?)

While researching the concepts of soft and strong, I looked up "soft skills":

- creative thinking
- leadership skills
- networking
- teamwork
- conflict resolution
- empathy
- sense of humor
- self-control
- positive attitude
- listening skills
- assertiveness
- adaptability
- emotional intelligence
- persuasion

The internet lists go on. As a behavior scientist I do not categorize people or actions this way, because it's extremely subjective and contextual, and it creates tunnel vision and bias. It also isn't very useful. But I came to find that soft skills are essentially an abstract spectrum of actions and traits that make you a human. Hard skills appear to be any concrete skill of value one might learn in order to excel at their job. Therefore, it may be more effective to refer to "human skills" and "work skills" and to value human skills first (because they are more important and more difficult to teach, theoretically) and the more concrete and easily taught work skills second. If we could think this way instead, would we be better at hiring "for culture"? Would women dominate promotion metrics if traits like empathy, listening, and creativity were at the top of the Most Wanted at Work list? Would more people from every gender get better at demonstrating them?

What if we threw out *any* binary categorizations, which tend to force us into polarizing categories such as good vs. bad or valuable vs. less valuable, and simply defined individuals and their actions in terms of their unique attributes instead of binary Glass Boxes? Would we be better at choosing partners? At teaching our children about the world? At showing up as the truest, most authentic version of ourselves?

Celebrity trainer, model, and former ballet dancer Jason Wimberly is this concept embodied. In a recent conversation, we discussed strength, authenticity, and how the Glass Box phenomenon affects us all.

Jason, known for rocking a pair of heels down the NYFW runway *like a boss,* explained his struggles as a man in the hyper-masculine fitness world. Even after he gained traction and fame from his signature fitness methods and memorable TV appearances, some male fitness brands once interested in signing him ultimately decided to go in a "more masculine" direction.

"I thought, *I'm strong, I'm well respected in this field.* I was confused about what the issue was. So I strapped a heart monitor to my chest and taught four classes back to back. I beat the younger, 'more masculine' trainers every time. I realized it wasn't about strength; it was about the *perception* of strength. You have to be *strong* to strut in heels, girl! So I wear heels. So what? I also bench press two hundred pounds and spend time camping in nature. I'm very much a man. I just happen to like things other people consider feminine."

Luckily, brands like Kate Hudson's Fabletics and celebrities Jane Lynch and Selma Blair, in addition to his incredible friends, helped him form a place of belonging.

"Growing up, I was always mistaken for a girl—I was skinny *and* I was born with these cheekbones and lips. There was *no* hiding the fact that I was going to be an effeminate gay man. I didn't have a choice but to own it."

I pressed, curious. "But what helped you own it?"

"I just always found people I could be myself around."

That statement was everything, and I would reframe it to say that he *attracted* people he could be himself around. He developed his *Fuckless*ness from a young age by refusing to be contained in a Glass Box, and as a result, he attracted people who accepted and appreciated him for who he naturally is. I experienced this firsthand. When I first met Jason at one of his LA rooftop workouts, I immediately noticed the vibe of people who attended, from all walks of life, fitness levels, and places in the country. Everyone was accepting, grounded, and friendly. No offense, LA, but the city isn't exactly known for its friendly community feel. Yet there we were. I made friends I still have to this day.

When the world tells us, "Here's who you are. Be this," and we respond, "No, honey, I'm *this*," with a power stance and smile included, we make our truth abundantly clear: who we are is not up for discussion or change. Jason made it abundantly clear that he was going to be a person who wore a full face of makeup and heels, danced ballet, bench pressed hundreds of pounds, and also happened to be a man who dated other men. Period. Next topic. He wasn't going to say no to the things he wanted to do, wear, think, or say simply because he possessed a penis. As a result, he is the person people enjoy so much today.

But what about all the incredibly unique, diverse, and interesting women out there who want the same for themselves but who are pressured into believing that their strength and desires are wrong? How else are we missing out? *Who* else are we missing out on by continuing to hand off this antiquated, socially ineffective fuck?

The upheaval of the past several years has started a critical strength renaissance. We are now aware enough to perceive acts of authenticity, vulnerability, compassion, humility, and emotional maturity as strong, but we must also continue to build a society that *rewards* this behavior in *all* individuals. Not only for the health of women—and men who happen to rock a pair of heels—but for the health of society.

In 2020, Landon Donovan—arguably one of the most well-known male American soccer players of all time and someone I'm lucky enough to call a friend and former client—led his team in an unprecedented walkout, forfeiting the playoffs, due to a homophobic slur directed at one of his players. On the video replay, you can hear the back-and-forth among the coaches and referee, which provides a stellar example of attempted punishment for this modern version of strength.

Landon said, "This is beyond soccer."

The opposing coach attempted to punish this move of strength and hand off Fucks #1 and #5: "Come on, man. Don't make a big scene."

"We have to get this out of our game!" Landon insisted.

"They're competing."

"It's homophobic!"

"How long have you been playing soccer?!" (Another attempted punishment by the opposing coach.)

Landon responded, "You're better than that."

When I called Landon to get his thoughts on the event for this chapter, he said that some fruitful conversations arose from the situation and that he thought many people had learned from it. I asked him if he received any backlash for sticking up for his player.

"Some people suggested I could've been less emotional about it, but generally, I was supported. I do wish I was more composed, but the result would've been the same."

My ears perked, and I smiled. Fuck #5 (Be Stifled) in action.

"And those who suggested you could have been less emotional, did they happen to be men?"

"I knew you were going to say that! Yes, they were men," he said with a laugh.

From where I sat, I didn't see an overly emotional man losing his shit on the field. I saw someone who was rightfully angry that a young man was called an extremely hurtful and pejorative name under the guise of "competition" and who leveraged his authority and leadership status to highlight an injustice. He wasn't angry at the opposing player or the coach. He was angry at a *system,* a view of strength and competition, that needs to change.

I became extra heated and curious (a.k.a. "passionate") about the topic. I had to make a point.

"Do you think the message would've been as powerful if you weren't emotional? If you'd calmly said, 'That's not very nice,' and simply walked away?"

"Probably not, no."

That event went viral and spread like wildfire, including to *Good Morning America,* where millions watched the story replay. I truly believe it changed some things permanently, and at the very least, it gave other men in sports an example of what genuine strength in leadership looks like.

The modern definition of strength may also include self-compassion. When Landon took a four-month break from his career in 2013 (citing the preservation of his mental health as the primary reason), he received some incredible backlash. "People just wanted me to shut up and play soccer. It was incredibly heavy."

When I mentioned it sounded very much like Simone Biles's decision to withdraw from some events at the 2020 Summer Olympic Games, he said, "Exactly, yes. She was also afraid she was going to get hurt. And I was afraid I would hurt myself in another way. If I had said I was taking four months off to nurse an injury, it wouldn't have been a big deal. But because I was taking care of my mental health, it was viewed as something I should continue to push through. This not only speaks to how we view strength, but also to (how we view) mental and physical health."

His comment brought to mind the day Meghan Markle and Prince Harry decided to create space from the royal family. The backlash was horrid. The assumption that Markle was acting selfishly, "leaving all the tiaras and fame," was sad to watch. I also noticed that while the couple eventually said it was the prince who made the call, Markle took the brunt of the blame and anger. As a powerful and strong woman of color, she was handed the heaviest and harshest words from those raised on Fucks #1 and #2—that women should be small and soft, and therefore nice and liked—above all else, even their own health.

This was a *values* call. If Meghan and Harry—or Simone Biles and Landon Donovan, for that matter—valued fame and wealth over their own health, they wouldn't have chosen to uproot their lives and face certain societal and media recoil in the process.

These examples show the modern kind of strength needed in leadership and society, regardless of gender. This is how culture is altered. It gives permission and sets in stone a new, more effective way of operating.

Are you interested in raising a female with the ability to independently navigate her life and achieve her goals?

She will need strong, confident, *Fuckless*, kick-the-door-down skills to make it. She will need the courage, bravery, resilience, and resolve to stay strong on the playground and in the boardroom.

Are you interested in climbing ladders? In traveling the world? In dropping other people's opinions to live a life of your making?

You will need those strong, confident, *Fuckless*, kick-the-door-down skills to make it. You will need the courage, bravery, resilience, and resolve to stay strong in the boardroom and in the world.

Strong is hard. I know you've shown your power and strength through your passion, excitement, or effort, and I know it's been dismissed and overlooked by someone who was uncomfortable with it. I am sorry you had that experience. It is always unfair when circumstances cause us shame or guilt for simply being ourselves. But continuing to be strong is necessary, empowering, and pretty goddamn helpful if you're navigating a life full of risks, as most of us are.

Telling young girls and women that they should be soft and easy creates tension and opposition between "soft" and the current definition of strength I've been discussing.

By "strong," I mean advocating for yourself and others on the basis of your beliefs, values, feelings, and knowledge in a respectful manner. I mean taking agency, being independent, and saying or doing something because it aligns with what you know to be true and right for you. "Strong" is not coercion. It's not anti-societal behavior or yelling. It's not aggression and bullying, and it's not malicious. If you read the last two sentences and thought, *I do that*, you have some rethinking to do, because you might be acting according to someone else's version of strength.

We cannot successfully drop this fuck—the false narrative that tells us strong is not feminine, but aggressively masculine—until we consider two critical questions:

1. What is *your* definition of female or feminine?

2. How do you define strength within that context?

Go ahead and jot down some ideas of your definition that come to mind while you're digesting this section, or come back later once you've marinated a little:

• To me, feminine/female means:

....

....

....

- And I show this by:

....

....

....

Until we as a society can start *overtly* treating certain behavior as weak (e.g., aggression, yelling, gaslighting) and certain behavior as strong (e.g., vulnerability, communication, empathy, honesty), we will continue to fail at changing the narrative and the behaviors that occur as a result of this stagnant social norm. Anyone who has ever had to exercise self-restraint, emotional regulation, and effective and calm communication knows that this requires significantly more strength than bullying, fighting, or the like.

And this fuck hits every aspect of our lives.

When I worked for the Central Office of Special Education, I led a team of psychologists, speech pathologists, physical therapists, and occupational therapists in a $10 million state-of-the-art early childhood evaluation center located outside the Capitol building in Washington, DC. One of my tasks was to run the meeting during which the results of a child's evaluation were presented to the parents or caregivers. We typically concluded the meeting by determining the school and classroom in which the child would receive services such as speech or behavioral therapy.

The evaluations and reporting took weeks, and I was highly skilled at synthesizing information across a number of observations and assessments. I took great care to check findings with my own evaluations and review prior records to ensure I was placing the child in the best environment for their current level of functioning as well as what I felt they could achieve given the right environment. In 2009, the city did not have a great setup for children with autism. I had worked with this population for years, and this weighed on me heavily. I started going out to visit the schools I was recommending and talking with the teachers. I did my best to simultaneously run the evaluation team on the front end and help consult with the classrooms (sneakily) on the back end.

One day I was pulled into my executive director's office. My director was also there. This would typically put the fear of God in an employee, but given that these were my favorite bosses to-date (and remain so), I was excited to hear what they had to say.

They told me they needed to bring me in to lead a meeting, and Meghan Koehler, one of the top educational attorneys in the district (and obviously not her real name), was the educational attorney.

My first thought was: *shit.*

But I said, "You got it."

I reviewed the report, evaluations, and recommendations written by my colleague. I was confident they were what was best for the child. This was pretty much the only rule in our startup-like department. I drafted documents, broke laws (little lame ones), and had immense purpose while guided by this rule. It was truly a Wild West time in my career and in the district, and I lived for it.

The bulk of the meeting is a blur to me now, but I remember being calmly challenged on every front. Having an attorney for a father, I recognized this tactic. It was meant to slowly wear me down and chip away at my confidence. This is where I developed my "pecked to death by a duck" metaphor. When I stated our recommendations, Ms. Koehler pressed harder and got more intense. She used her glasses, notebook, and pen as weapons of coercion—slamming her pen down and taking her glasses off in a quick, calculated manner that was supposed to signal I was in dangerous waters. Also a lesson from my father, I knew it was a signal she felt like she was losing control of the conversation. After she had made several attempts to sway my decision, I suggested we take a break. This would decrease the emotional intensity, derailing her tactic to force me to change my decision based on fear.

I calmly walked into my executive director's office. I explained the situation and confessed I wasn't sure what to do next.

"What do you think you should do?" my executive director asked me.

"These recommendations are what's best for the child."

"Okay," they said. "So go do that."

I thought, *Thanks for the sink-or-swim lesson.*

But I said, "You got it."

I reconvened the meeting. While everyone else in the room seemed to be calmer, I knew my next move was essentially pouring an ocean of gasoline on a forest fire. I reviewed the results in a quick summation.

"And due to the skill level, age, and diagnosis of the child, I will be sticking with our recommendation."

In response, Ms. Koehler threw her pen and notebook and slammed her glasses down. She also spewed lots of angry words masquerading as strength.

I leaned back in my chair and listened. After years of watching a certain type of man lose his temper when he was challenged or lost control—and being on the receiving end of this anger—I had learned to maintain emotional homeostasis. To this day, when someone raises their voice in anger, I feel calm. Crazy yelling is my lavender oil.

People who resort to this behavior are not strong. They are out of control, and they know it. My twenty-six-year-old self had just shut down one of the top educational attorneys in a city where people go to be attorneys. And I did what was best for a child in the process. That day, I learned what strength was. Of course, I struggled and regressed and failed to consistently demonstrate this skill over the next twelve years (and counting), so I hope you refrain from thinking this process was or is easy.

I have similar stories that involve men, but I wanted to tell this story for three reasons:

1. *All* genders have been given a skewed picture of what strength looks like. We can't simply smash the patriarchy. We must bring all genders together to discuss the past and redefine the future in regard to strength and leadership.
2. I must admit the attorney's behavior was much more offensive coming from a woman. I would have expected it from a man but was aghast that a woman would treat me that way. We are all works in progress, and I struggle with this fuck every day.
3. This example tees up our next discussion on the "double bind" challenge women face.

The "double bind" or "assertiveness penalty" finds that women who demonstrate leadership characteristics like assertiveness are significantly less liked than their male counterparts who behave the same way. In a 2018 study published in *Psychological Science*, women who showed anger at work were perceived as less competent, received lower wages, and received a lower perceived status. Men who demonstrated anger received a *boost* in their perceived status.

Sounds like a whole lot of socio-normative fucks to me.

While briefly dating a man internationally known for his leadership books, talks on empathy and purpose, and being a good human, I found a note in his nightstand from another woman he was clearly involved with. I wasn't snooping. He absentmindedly asked me to get something in there (and he happened to be tied up and blindfolded at the time). When I calmly showed it to him, he erupted. He began yelling, gaslighting me into believing I was ridiculous to even question him. For clarity, this was the third woman we'd had to discuss in as many weeks.

He grabbed my arm and pulled me into his bathroom while continuing to yell at me. Watching him, I was amazed. His performance was perfect. If I were a less experienced woman, I actually would've believed I was in the wrong for doubting him. I remained calm with my Snake Oil Salesman. Unfortunately for him, I was 100 percent immune to this strategy and saw it for what it was: gaslighting, an admission of guilt and, quite frankly, basic immaturity. I left his house and never returned. However, through narcissist-level anger or theatrical speeches, society will continue to reward this behavior in one gender over another.

True strength involves noticing our emotional states and personal agendas and then rethinking our stance or dropping our ego to consider facts, logic, and other people's ideas. We need to clearly define and value "strength" regardless of gender so we can all move forward together.

Many women I know are ambitious, tenacious, and hard working. They fight for respect because they have been put in the position to defend who they naturally are in order to earn it. I also know many family-oriented women who do not want the same things as more career-oriented women. They settled down early, got married, left the workforce, and had children. That is *lovely*, and I would absolutely call it strong. They run the household, organize the lives of everyone in the family, and somehow manage to cook healthy dinners while keeping everyone happy and alive. It pains me that these women are not traditionally seen and valued as strong.

This isn't about judgment. It's about accepting and encouraging varieties of women just as we should accept and encourage varieties of men. It's about taking the notion of feminine as soft and the notion of masculine as strong and questioning the utility of it. Are we doing right by ourselves to continue to condition each other this way? If we redefine strength, are women stronger?

Consider what it would be like to stop accepting other people's fucks about the propriety of your strength or softness, and simply own wherever you are. Your strength, in whatever form it exists, is yours, and you can (and do) possess both strength and softness.

Accept it. Love it. Leverage it.

Strong.

Strong.

Strong.

Strong.

My softness and my strength are one.

Fuck
Being Soft

Consider with curiosity:

- When and with whom is being soft rewarded?
- When and with whom is being your version of strength rewarded?
- Where did your story of soft come from?
- What is maintaining it and what are you getting from it?
- What is likely to happen if you keep this fuck?

YOUR REWRITE

In the following exercise, fill in the blanks when you feel inspired and clear. You can choose to commit to these new beliefs any time you're ready.

1. I'm dropping the belief that

....

....

2. Because

....

....

3. If I'm successful, (what will happen?)

....

....

4. If I'm successful, I will have time and energy for

....

....

5. And it will feel

....

....

6. My new belief is

....

....

7. And I will show this by (be specific: actions, words, phrases, etc.)

....

....

fuck #3

Be Less

"*They'd say I hustled, put in the work*

They wouldn't shake their heads and question how much of this I deserve

What I was wearing, if I was rude

Could all be separated from my good ideas and power moves...

I'm so sick of running as fast as I can

Wondering if I'd get there quicker if I was a man."

—TAYLOR SWIFT, "THE MAN"

In addition to the world defining femininity as small and soft, women continue to receive the message that they are less valuable, trustworthy, or capable than their male counterparts, even when they achieve the same things.

In a *Wall Street Journal* op-ed, the second-worst Epstein tears into Dr. Jill Biden for a title she rightfully earned. The infantilization started with a demoralizing, belittling tone and continued by reducing her education:

> Madame First Lady—Mrs. Biden—Jill—kiddo: a bit of advice on what may seem like a small but I think not unimportant matter. Any chance you might drop the "Dr." before your name? "Dr. Jill Biden" sounds and feels fraudulent, not to say a touch comic. Your degree is, I believe, an Ed.D., a doctor of education...A wise man once said that no one should call himself "Dr." unless he has delivered a child. Think about it, Dr. Jill, and forthwith drop the doc.

I can all but guarantee that this small-dick energy would have never been, and to my knowledge has never been, publicly directed toward a man. If the contributor, who I won't even mention by full name, truly wanted to expose "fraudulent" use of the doctor title, he might be interested to learn that Dr. Phil obtained his PhD in clinical psychology with a dissertation on rheumatoid arthritis and has, to my knowledge, never delivered a child. Yet he's earned fame and wealth by solving problems on national television under his doctor title for decades without incurring infantilizing op-eds from washed-up writers. Simon Sinek once spouted basic neuroscience and its possible correlation to leadership but holds only a bachelor's in cultural anthropology. No babies delivered, no advanced degree, and no problem cultivating a following of millions. Adam Grant, exponentially more skilled and talented in the area of leadership and organizational psychology, does incredible work under his PhD title, but also has yet to deliver a baby. (I'd be remiss not to mention that he was one of the most notable male academics to come to Dr. Jill Biden's side, defending her and her work when lesser men couldn't handle it.)

On the subject of important roles and the degrees of people in those roles, the writer might have also mentioned the fact that our former Secretary of Education, Betsy DeVos, had but a bachelor's degree in business administration and political science and that her Wikipedia page seems to purposely bury information on her education (but makes several mentions of the wealth and accomplishments of her father, brother, and husband).

Dr. Jill Biden, and many other PhDs in the female-dominated field of education, was publicly attacked for what I can only assume to be simply existing in the world as an educated and powerful woman. This is not only gender-based intellectual oppression; it's a prime example of the notion that women are simply *less*.

Research shows that women tend to be interrupted in meetings more frequently than men and that their ideas receive attention more frequently when echoed through a male colleague. Significantly more women than men report that doctors have brushed aside their pain or worry as if it were overreactive. The gender pay gap still remains. People question women more than men at nearly every opportunity.

In the aforementioned research by Adam Grant, males received higher performance evaluations and were perceived as helpful when they contributed valuable ideas, but females who contributed equally were not given the same high rating of performance or helpfulness. Research from the corporate world continues to reinforce these findings. While a 2019 article from the *Harvard Business Review* shows that women rate *higher* than men in most leadership skills, less than 8 percent of Fortune

500 companies have female leaders, and this is at a record high in 2021.

During the San Diego Women's March following the Most Fucked Election of All Time, I marched next to signs that said, "I've been fighting since the '70s" and "I can't believe I'm still marching for this shit." Preach! We've undoubtedly seen progress, but if it were enough, you wouldn't be holding this book. I harbor fantasies of forehead-poking people who respond to gender inequality with comments like, "Well, there are women CEOs now." *So what?* Victory? We can all go home now? Everything is cool? This is the same logic as saying there are black CEOs so racism can't really be a thing anymore either. Did you know that in early 2016, there were more CEOs named John than women CEOs in total? As of 2019, the male-to-female CEO ratio was nineteen to one.

We are not anywhere near cool.

I can't tell you how many times I've heard things like, "I'd promote a woman, but they just don't speak up. They don't ask for what they want." As soon as forty-eight hours later, I am sure to hear, "I finally put my idea on the table today, and it only got attention when a male repeated it," or "I finally took your advice and spoke up, but he completely ignored me," from a female friend. Again, it's that double-bind assertiveness penalty at play.

How is someone supposed to behave when they are told one thing and then the opposite—and then, no matter what, they are wrong or ignored anyway?

This is the Glass Box in action. I am honestly shocked there aren't more women going on murderous rampages because they are made to feel like they're taking a daily dose of crazy pills. *That* is emotional control.

While conducting interviews for this book, I spoke with Alex, a transgender doctor and the former boss of a friend. Over the course of a touching, enlightening, two-hour discussion, he told me his story of being assigned the female gender at birth, his experiences as a female, and how he came to transition to being male. When I asked him to share the biggest differences in how people treated him before and after transitioning, he said, "I absolutely experience more privilege as a man. All of a sudden, people started to defer to me in meetings, whether I actually knew what I was talking about or not."

In effect, he became more important. More capable. More trustworthy.

In every single interview I conducted for this book, the theme of women as "less than" surfaced, meaning that when it comes to the workplace or society, a story exists that women are not as valuable or important as men. Even when overt behavior suggests women are heard, like when a company publicizes a gender equality stance, the actions that follow typically show that women continue to remain overlooked, not trusted, or not taken as seriously as their male counterparts.

Some of the comments I heard included:

"My female boss kept asking me when I would have children. It started to get really uncomfortable. It was as if it was the only thing she saw when she looked at me."

"I had an idea, and it was dismissed. Moments later my male colleague said the same thing, and it received praise and acknowledgment. I felt like I was taking crazy pills. No one even noticed."

"I have to be a completely different person in the boardroom, from how I walk to how I speak, to be taken seriously at all."

"My friend, a single dad, began complaining about how hard it is to juggle his child and work and about how paternity leave is minimal in his company. He never once mentioned anything about how women juggle these things all the time while being expected to produce the same as the men in their office. It was as if women had been blindly complaining about this same struggle for decades, but now that he was experiencing it, it was important."

Barack Obama was the first president in history to call himself a feminist. Still, two-thirds of his first-term top aides were men. His female aides, feeling the frustration of being interrupted or of having their ideas restated and acknowledged by men, developed a system called "amplification." The premise was simple: *become vocal; become visible; become valuable.* When a female aide made a key point or shared a good idea, another female aide would repeat it and give credit to the woman who first shared it. It provided the women with the additional visibility needed to highlight the issue and the solution. It had long-term consequences and gained the attention of the president, who made specific points to call on more (and sometimes *only*) women.

Fantastic. But how did we land here in the first place? Why the fuck do we still have to fight so hard to be treated like humans with value?

As the late Ruth Bader Ginsberg put it:

> When I'm sometimes asked when will there be enough [women on the Supreme Court] and I say, "When there are nine," people are shocked. But there'd been nine men, and nobody's ever raised a question about that.

It evades the scope of this book to evaluate the other influencing variables to women in leadership, such as caregiving responsibilities, lack of appropriate mentorship, very little visibility of female representation at the top, and few pipelines solely dedicated to tracking women (and minorities, for that matter) to leadership positions. But we can all agree that this fuck is not holding only women back; it's holding us all back.

If we have fewer women and minorities and less diversity in general at the decision-making level, we go against what we know to be true about innovation.

An article published in *Proceedings in the National Academy of Sciences* stated the following:

> Guided by key research findings, we propose the following "mechanisms for innovation" specifying why gender diversity matters for scientific discovery and what managers should do to maximize its benefits. Encouraging greater diversity is not only the right thing to do; it allows scientific organizations to derive an "innovation dividend" that leads to smarter, more creative teams, hence opening the door to new discoveries.

My favorite study on innovation and diversity included two groups, one composed of white male scientists and one of scientists from various racial, gender, and age groups. They were both given the same problem to solve, and each group came up with equally solid, effective answers. However, the group of white males came up with significantly fewer solutions than the diverse group. This makes sense. How many similar brains, educational backgrounds, and learning histories do we benefit from if innovation is the mission?

It's also been shown that women don't value *each other*. In 1983, the Hollywood Directors Guild sued the production studios for discrimination, as a shocking minority of the directors were women and it was apparent there were specific career barriers in place for them. They were assigned a female judge and thought lived experience was on their side. But in a surprising turn of events, the judge threw out the case. She made the point that the small percentage of female directors who *did* exist were also discriminatory because they *also* did not hire females!

I can attest to this in my own life. I have never known any of my girlfriends to talk business and hire one another, whereas I've watched many of my male friends discuss business and money-making collaborations under any condition involving beer and a few snacks. They naturally trust each other, and women don't—we are taught from a surprisingly young age to see each other as either less valuable and trustworthy or as competition (more on that later).

When women are interrupted, overlooked, and treated as decoration in the boardroom, everyone loses. They speak up less. They contribute less. They throw their hat in the ring for promotions less. They add less value to your company, and they burn out faster because their existence in the workplace requires five times more effort (or at least a few other women echoing everything they say before people realize they are speaking). If women are shown to be equal or better leaders, have innovative ideas, exercise excellent detail orientation, and be great collaborators, why are they continuously treated as though they are less valuable than their counterparts?

In your search for a solution to feeling right, worthy, or acceptable, have you ever purchased expensive clothes, blown money on blowouts, dated people who mistreated you, overeaten, drank too much, or vented to friends while wishing the world would just *value you for who you naturally are?* Of course you have. Because while it's hard enough to continuously demand to be as valued as men, it's exhausting to do while being second-guessed and questioned incessantly. This all happens concurrent with society wondering why women hesitate or need validation to make decisions at work and in life.

It is *maddening.*

So you buy the books, listen to the podcasts, and follow the women who appear to have risen above the noise because it's easier than facing hard truths and making big changes in your daily reality.

Well, I'm here to tell you that it's easier, but it's not better. Trust me. I tried it for three decades.

I started innocently enough. When I was ten, I proclaimed, righteously and with conviction, that my dreams were to become a pediatrician *and* own a donut shop. I noticed the donut shop idea received laughs of dismissal. I also noticed my pediatrician dream was met with acceptance, smiles, and comments like, "Oh, you must be a very smart little girl, then."

I equated "pediatrician" with "smart" and "donut shop owner" with "not good enough."

That was circa 1992.

Fast forward to 2009, when I was attending George Washington University for graduate school. I had written for a few magazines and was honing my academic writing skills while also maintaining my journaling practice. I decided that I would continue with graduate school but that I also wanted to become a writer. It fueled me and energized me like nothing else ever had.

I bought some books on how to get published and how to write for a certain audience. To be accountable for this (unknowingly lifelong) dream, I told people about it.

Mistake #1.

"Aren't you in graduate school for something different, though?"

"Oh, don't be silly. That's not a career."

"It is very hard to become a writer."

"Publishing a book is a lot of work."

"I don't know. I just don't see that for you."

While the words sounded different, the message by which the news was delivered always sounded the same.

I heard:

"You are not good enough."

"That's silly."

"You want too much."

"That is simply the wrong way to live your life."

"What I want for you is right. What you want for yourself is wrong."

When my rescue pup, Olivia Chewton John, began showing signs of a neurological issue, I went to a vet. Then another vet. Then a friend who is a vet. Regardless of gender, I was dismissed at every opportunity. The message was, "Calm down. You don't know what you're talking about." Then I remembered, I'm a badass behavior analyst paid to notice things other people don't. Why the fuck did I need permission to get my dog the tests I thought she needed? I pushed.

Meningitis.

If she'd gone another few months, she likely wouldn't have made it.

Several months later, there was a bump on my other rescue, Franklin. I took him to the vet and said it looked like it had grown just the smallest bit.

"We'll watch it. Don't worry about it right now," she said.

"Nah, let's worry about it," I said. "Please test him."

Cancer.

Quick surgery, and it was gone.

When I posted a screenshot of my Tesla order, a girlfriend texted to ask, "Are you *sure* you want a Tesla?"

When I told my financial advisor (and very good friend) I was going to make the move back East, he said "Are you *sure?*"

When I put ranch dressing on my salad a few weeks ago, a friend said, "Are you *sure?* I thought your stomach reacted to dairy."

If I could pull off a "Yes, I'm fucking sure" tattoo on my face, I'd do it, just to save the energy of having to explain myself.

While the above experiences may be annoying, there are also some very serious side effects to the survival of the fuck that tells us women are not to be taken seriously, that they are less valuable, and that they are mistaken about what they experience, think, and feel.

Nearly 80 percent of rape and sexual assaults are not reported. Survivors are second-guessed and questioned so frequently that many don't believe they will be heard. This narrative is so strongly implanted in women that most survivors even question *themselves* at some point.

A woman I've known for years, and who wishes to remain anonymous, shared with me her first heartbreaking experience of being dismissed by her father. His best friend had sexually abused her for years, starting when she was fifteen years old. When she told her father, he told her she was mistaken. Her next three relationships were with men who were much older, manipulative, and sexually abusive. She suffers from PTSD and remains largely untrusting of people to this day.

Also during her formative years, this woman's next-door neighbor started harassing her and watching her through her bedroom window. Again, she told her father. Again, he downplayed it as though she was somehow making it up or mistaken. It was not until he caught the man, who didn't know her father was home, that he believed it to be true. It took three years. In the process, she learned to hide and navigate around his work schedule and was otherwise a prisoner in her own bedroom.

This tragic phenomenon shows up in healthcare and romantic relationships too. Though much less severe than the previous story, I've experienced it in my own life.

At first, I tried not to let the pain show. I began to see spots, which meant life was about to get exponentially worse. As the nausea hit me, I stood up to walk to my bathroom but collapsed on the floor after several steps. The pain was agonizing. All I could do was writhe on the ground and try to distract myself until it was over.

My then-husband (and several doctors) never took it seriously, so I learned to stay quiet until it passed. Then, during the worst physical pain of my life, I was lucid enough to calmly wonder where my husband was. I looked up. He was still standing at our farmhouse sink, doing the dishes and watching me, emotionless. He wasn't concerned. He wasn't scared. He wasn't unhappy. He was just…blank. The scientist in me was curious about this behavior.

"This is when you come and comfort your *wife*," I gasped through my tears.

He slowly put a dish down and walked over, plunking down next to me for a few seconds until I crawled into our bathroom and vomited.

I suffer from endometriosis. Each month, instead of normal monthly cramps, I essentially go into labor for about six hours. The condition causes me so much pain that I see spots, lie on the floor crying, and occasionally vomit. Of all the things I've tried—CBD oil, pain meds, heating pads, and the like—the tried-and-true method of survival is a good stiff drink (so if you ever see me tipsy on a Tuesday morning, don't judge).

I have had this condition since I was a teenager, only I never knew it because my mother, who experienced the same pain her entire life, told me "We just get bad cramps." Not until I was thirty-six did I receive a diagnosis. Even though I had rolled myself off my bed in pain (a few times), cried to the point of screaming (I'd broken bones without shedding a tear), and even scared a college roommate so badly that she carried me to her car and sped to the hospital, no one took this pain seriously. No one believed it was bad enough, so I didn't believe it was bad enough. I suffered for twenty years—missing parties, work, and other events in the process.

For some reason, after that particular episode that left me borderline catatonic with pain, I asked my husband why he didn't come to comfort me on his own accord. He said he would take some time to think about it. A few days later, he texted me:

"It just seemed like you really wanted attention."

My words and feelings weren't taken seriously. They were dismissed because if a woman is experiencing it, she is probably just being dramatic. Millions of other women share this story; many of them tell of going from doctor to doctor and, regardless of the physician's gender, being treated as though they are bothersome and complaining about nothing.

Ever dealt with "man flu"? Then you know where I'm going with this. Somehow, women's needs just don't count, but when men have the same (or markedly less severe) experiences, the outcome is very different.

This experience continues beyond medical conditions and grounds itself in the daily lives of nearly every woman on the planet.

It's the mental and emotional sludge we women must walk through in the process of making things happen.

The second-guessing.

The message that we are somehow wrong or silly for wanting what we want.

The tone that our desires are not valuable enough to invest in.

The numbers of women in entertainment and business who receive markedly less funding for equally viable ideas and companies.

The assumption that when we talk about what we want for ourselves, it is open for criticism.

Exhausting.

Over and over, women are told:

"It can't be that bad."

"Women are too emotional."

"Women are angry."

"Women are bitter."

"Men are just more controlled and less crazy."

But at the same time, women are also told:

"Women don't speak up."

"Women don't ask for things."

"Men are just more assertive."

From these mixed messages, women learn:

You are not taken seriously.

You can't trust yourself.

You are invisible.

You are not seen or heard.

You, your skills, and your experiences are less important.

To anyone with whom this resonates, this is the perfect moment to drop this fuck. You are not asking for a handout; you are simply asking to be seen and considered to be as valuable as your male counterparts. You are not blaming others for everything you're not; you are simply expecting those around you to see you as capable of making decisions about your own life.

Consider what it might feel like to wake up every day feeling the unbridled power of true equality. Of living in a way that sends a clear, unapologetic message: that your thoughts, ideas, desires, and lifestyle hold value, without question or sidebar.

My femininity is not a disqualifier.

Fuck
Being Less

Consider with curiosity:

- When and with whom do you feel invisible or untrustworthy?
- When and with whom do you feel valuable, empowered, and important?
- Where did your story of being less come from?
- What is maintaining it, and what are you getting from it?
- What is likely to happen if you keep this fuck?

YOUR REWRITE

In the following exercise, fill in the blanks when you feel inspired and clear. You can choose to commit to these new beliefs any time you're ready.

1. I'm dropping the belief that

....

....

2. Because

....

....

3. If I'm successful, (what will happen?)

....

....

4. If I'm successful, I will have time and energy for

....

....

5. And it will feel

....

....

6. My new belief is

....

....

7. And I will show this by (be specific: actions, words, phrases, etc.)

....

....

Be the Exception

"*No country can ever truly flourish if it stifles the potential of its women and deprives itself of the contribution of half its citizens.*"

—MICHELLE OBAMA

Despite the fact that women make up the majority of the workforce (and the world), the language around gender continues to qualify women as a small subset of both. Phrases like "girl boss," "women's leadership event," or "female CEO" strengthen the rhetoric that women are the exception to a role typically reserved for males. By discussing leadership and other titles with gender qualifiers, we silo women apart from the roles in which they so rightfully belong. We also show young girls that these women are the exception, not the rule, reinforcing a world where this is the way it is instead of the way it used to be.

Women are not a side dish; we are 52 percent of the main course.

In the documentary *This Changes Everything*, Geena Davis discusses her efforts to eliminate gender bias and elevate women through changes in entertainment and media. As it turns out, when the movies *Hunger Games* and *Raya and the Last Dragon* hit the public, girls began signing up for archery in droves. Signups skyrocketed over 100 percent, passing adult males. This is known as the CSI Effect: what people see on their screens affects real-life scenarios.

When young girls and women can see it's possible—even in the movies—it becomes possible *for them.*

In 2019, I was invited to sit on a panel at a leadership summit for behavior scientists. The title of the panel was "Women in Leadership." While on stage, my fellow colleagues and I were asked the question, "What can we do to change the landscape of leadership for females, and how can we use behavior analysis to do so?"

We had known the question was coming, and it was decided that I would be the one to state the obvious, but uncomfortable, answer:

"We need to stop using qualifiers like 'Women in Leadership Panel' as if women are the minority. We are a field of 86 percent women."

I looked out into the crowd and noticed a few open-mouthed, "aha moment" faces as the point landed.

I continued to make the following point:

Our verbal behavior is important because it sends signals about what is expected and what is outside the norm. Women are not the minority, but we are continuously treated as a smaller subset of individuals. Even if an executive team is less than 50 percent female, do we really want to start infantilizing women by calling them "women leaders" or "female CEOs"? Why not just "our CEO"?

Consider this example from the sports world: Tennis star Andy Murray had just lost his Wimbledon title to Sam Querrey and was in a conversation with the press when he made a major callout.

An *Insider* article recounted the scenario:

> Querrey had become the first male tennis player [from the US] to reach a Grand Slam semi-final since 2009, though in that time a host of female players have gone further, most notably 23-time champion Serena Williams. A journalist said to Murray: "Sam is the first US player to reach a major semi-final since 2009," before the 30-year-old took him to task. "Male player," Murray said.

This is the kind of gentle correction and mindfulness we need from all genders, all the time, to continue dropping the societal fuck that women are the exception or, in this case, just plain invisible.

We also use this language as it relates to race. This is one more example of how "normal" orbits around not just men, but specifically white men.

When we say "black CEO" or "female CEO," we view life through the lens that anyone but a white male is "other," and, therefore, not the norm. And this goes *much* further than CEOs (depending on the CEO).

Have you ever noticed that we assume that creatures like insects and animals are male? We say, "Look at that little guy go! He sure is fast!" And in grammar—when I was in eighth grade English class, I vividly remember being told that "he" was the assumed pronoun and used throughout literature. This always bothered me. I felt offended and excluded and thought, *Why are boys so important?* Over twenty years later, while sitting at a cafe in Stockholm reading a leadership book, I was officially over it. I began drawing an "s" in front of every "he," so I could read the content as if it applied to me at all.

One of my colleagues and a dear friend—let's call her Sophie—and I had spent the night before the Women in Leadership panel discussing the event and our feelings about the way gender plays out in our field. She said, "So Bob (the main organizer, and not his real name) wants to open with a story about how having a daughter made him want to help women in our field." I cringed. We hear men say this all the time.

What is said: "Having a daughter made me care about women's issues. I want her to grow up with the same opportunities a man would have."

This is a great start. But we hear: "Upon creating something from my own loins and thus having a reason to care, I realized women are humans too."

What about your wife? Your sister? Your mother? Your female friends? People who do not share your lineage or chromosomes, but the women all around you currently fighting to be taken seriously, for a fair shot, to be seen and heard?

I asked Sophie what she said. "I suggested he not and tried to explain how it would come off. He said he didn't care because it was true." He indeed opened with the line, followed by a hearty pat on the back for the two men, who he mentioned by name (one being himself), who gave up some of their minutes so "the women's panel" would have more time on stage.

This impressed people in the audience, but Sophie, ever the epic analyst, ran the numbers. For every hour a man was given to speak, women were (originally) given six minutes. I believe our extra time bumped this to nine minutes or so. The presenters, all but one of them men, conducted their talks that morning. Sophie continued to keep track of how many women and men were mentioned by name.

Men: Twenty.

Women: Eleven.

On several occasions, in place of a woman's name a male speaker said "a female colleague," "one of the female directors," or "one of the women on the women's panel" (I shit you not. That's not even time-efficient). There were exactly *zero times* someone mentioned a male in the same manner, such as "one of the male researchers" or "one of my male colleagues."

We had both spoken to our male peers about the topic of women in leadership before and after the event. It amused me to hear things like: "I don't have anything against women, but I'm not going to hire a woman just to put her in a role," or "Women just don't do the work that men do," or that daughter thing again. I feel every man should understand why you might sound like a total dick (or completely ignorant, at best) by verbalizing these thoughts, but behavior analysts especially should know better than to completely discount the role our environment plays on things like rapport-building (i.e., relationship-building), or learning history (e.g., only seeing men in leadership roles and thus inferring leadership positions are solely for men), not to mention competing priorities (e.g., raising children). Moreover, these comments fail to consider the barriers to producing "the amount of work that men do," such as the significant mental loads women carry, additional household responsibilities, and other common attitudes by men in academia.

As a woman coming from a highly academic field, I can attest that this is unfortunately the norm—for now. Due to the environments in which academics work and the staunch bureaucratic frameworks that constructed them, it is extremely difficult for women to rise up in this field, not to mention be taken as seriously as our male counterparts.

Along with being siloed and sidelined, we receive the message that when we are thrown a bone, we should take it with a smile. During the same conference's lunch, one of the event staff approached our table and asked if we wanted to purchase a T-shirt. As she flashed us the front and back of the shirt, my eye caught something.

"Wait. Let me see the back, please," I requested.

And there it was: my name, along with the names of the other panelists, plastered without our knowledge or permission on products being sold.

I lost my cool.

"Oh, *what the fuck*," I said. The poor event staff member froze in position.

I looked at Sophie. Her eyes were wide as she took in the shirt.

Another (female) colleague was sitting with us. "I mean, at least he's promoting you!" she exclaimed.

And what she meant was, "Be happy you were mentioned."

I went on to explain the following as calmly as I could, given that the rabid-dog moment I wanted to have would have terrified her:

1. Putting someone's name on something they are selling without their consent or knowledge is total bullshit, not to mention illegal.
2. The failure to simply ask us for permission to use our names was a sign that the organizer knew it was wrong, didn't think about it, or felt entitled enough to use our names without feeling the need for permission. All of these are obvious and concerning missteps for someone who owns a large, very publicly marketed company.
3. In no way did I want to be associated with this company on a product. Not only are our companies completely different in their purpose and mission, but there are also strong incongruences between our values, branding, and messaging.

4. Neither Sophie nor I needed the publicity.

Bob stood on stage during his opening speech and said something to the effect of, "I am here to listen and to learn from the women on the panel today."

I would have liked to fact check this and quote him directly, but I received this response when I asked for a link to the recording of the event—something that we were told would be made available, as it was being livestreamed:

> Regarding the video, typically what happens is the video gets edited and brief YouTube/social media clips are made for those who approve of us doing so. We were under the impression you may not want to be in the videos due to your concerns over the T-shirt having your name on it and your announcement you did not like the name "Women in Leadership" panel.

This type of microaggression is typically called out in women as being passive-aggressive. I actually never said I didn't *like* the panel name; I simply made a point about the strength of pairing of words with gendered roles and the behavior that may result—a completely viable answer to the question I was asked. Additionally, while I also made no mention to anyone at the company about my name being used on the T-shirt (I had every intention and then lost the energy, and that's on me), they somehow knew how I felt but made no effort to share revenue or discuss the matter with anyone whose name appeared on the product without consent. They did, however, make sure we were not included or marketed in the videos of the conference we agreed to participate in.

Sophie calmly approached Bob for a discussion. She made note of the data and shared that she was upset her name was used. The organizer took out his phone to take a picture of the look of concern on her face, saying, "Stop being so angry. I want to show you how angry you look right now."

That really happened. Really.

It's hard for me to imagine that ridiculous action being carried out on a man. It must have been extremely embarrassing for Sophie to be on the receiving end of that type of ego-driven behavior when she was simply relaying information in order to educate someone who "wants to listen and learn" from women.

You might be thinking, *That's an honest mistake. It sounds like they meant well.* Should I receive a response to my email suggesting we chat about the matter in order to clear the air and learn from one another, I will be happy to adjust this section (at the time of writing, it has been over two years). Until then, I can only assume that these stories are recent examples of *genderwashing*.

In the green movement of the early 2000s, many companies started to make an effort to be more environmentally conscious. As with most initiatives that cost companies additional time, thought, and money, some bad apples began to cut corners. Thus, the phrase "greenwashing" was born. Defined as "disinformation disseminated by an organization so as to present an environmentally responsible public image," the term greenwashing gained attention and traction with those who were holding companies accountable for their claims.

It surprised me to find that genderwashing, while occasionally used in conversation, has not been properly defined or widely written about. In a 2016 *LiisBeth* article titled "The Seven Sins of Gender Washing," writer PK Mutch posited the following:

1. The Sin of Re-Skinning—A company that attempts to "look" like its work environment is currently gender progressive by ensuring its company website, annual report, and advertising copy has lots of women in the photos. It uses positive gender speak in its corporate communications, and content marketing output, yet when you check out the gender composition at the top it is 80 per cent, or worse, 100 per cent men.

2. The Sin of Worshipping False Progress—Where corporations create special "We Love Women Who Work Here" days; buy tickets to women empowerment lunches for female staff; appropriate initiatives like the UN's "HeforShe" campaign for commercial gain; or give to Oxfam's "I Am A Feminist" campaign as part of a marketing campaign, yet internal organizational policies and day-to-day gender-biased cultural practices remain fundamentally unchanged.

3. The Sin of Distraction—A claim suggesting the company is pro-gender equity, but upon digging deeper, you find the claim is based on a narrowly defined initiative without concern for the larger, more important issues. For example, in 2011, Walmart trumpeted its new Global Women's Economic Empowerment Initiative, which involved a commitment to source $20B from women-owned businesses. Sounds good, however, this amounts to just 5 per cent of its overall expenditures. And, Walmart was already buying from some women-owned firms. The initiative came on the heels of a class action suit launched against Walmart

by its 1.5 million female associates for its allegedly discriminatory practices.

4. The Sin of Inconsistency—Where distant head offices write, implement and impose gender equity and inclusion policies, and promote this as progress, but their branch plant or satellite operations in other jurisdictions don't follow suit and are not held accountable for doing so.

5. The Sin of Positioning Basic Compliance as Leadership—Companies that tout government-mandated policies—like pay equity or parental leave—as gender-progressive initiatives; or Ontario organizations that send out press releases announcing they "have done away with dress codes" (meanwhile dress codes have already been deemed unacceptable by the Ontario Human Rights Commission in 2016).

6. The Sin of Irrelevance—A case where a company promotes the fact that 65 per cent of its employees are women, however they are all on the factory floor, are mostly hired as part-time workers with no benefits, and have no representation in senior management let alone on the board.

7. The Sin of Only Counting Heads—A case where a company trumpets the addition of two new female board members or the promotion of a female manager to VP to change the ratio, not the culture. Sometimes, "non-trouble makers" or like-minded women who won't challenge the status quo are chosen by design. This does nothing to change the culture or support inclusion. Appointees we hope to see serve as changemakers become mere headstones at the board table, and their ability to create change for all genders in the company is amputated—usually at the voice.

These may sound familiar to you. They are common examples of Band-Aid solutions to larger problems that require deeper systemic solutions. It's genderwashing masquerading as authentic efforts to create equality for women.

The fire behind the resurgence of the women's movement seems to have separated individuals into two categories: those who calmly sit down to listen and understand from a point of curiosity and those who stand up and defend themselves out of fear and intimidation.

When a leader says, "I'm *not* just going to put a woman in a role because she's a woman," it highlights their fear that women are no longer tolerating being treated as the minority afterthought and that things are truly changing. To a man who has existed on little else than the fact that he pees standing up, this kind of change is threatening. I'm tempted to point out that it appears many men have been promoted on little more than their prowess on the golf course or penchant for local beer. It is the dream of my lifetime to see the day when business deals and promotions are conducted over champagne and spa days.

Or, of course, whatever you're into.

If you've been taught to accept that women and girls are to sit on the sidelines and be thankful for what they get, if you feel like you're existing on breadcrumbs and lip service at work or at home, if you have been siloed with qualifiers, or if you believe that you must wait your turn and play by the rules because you're lucky to be included with the boys, this could be a fuck to drop.

I will not accept a siloed existence
as an accessory to my womanhood.

Fuck Being the Exception

Consider with curiosity:

- When and with whom do you feel like an outcast?
- When and with whom do you feel included?
- Where did your story of being the exception come from?
- What is maintaining it, and what are you getting from it?
- What is likely to happen if you keep this fuck?

YOUR REWRITE

In the following exercise, fill in the blanks when you feel inspired and clear. You can choose to commit to these new beliefs any time you're ready.

1. I'm dropping the belief that

....

....

2. Because

....

....

3. If I'm successful, (what will happen?)

....

....

4. If I'm successful, I will have time and energy for

....

....

5. And it will feel

....

....

6. My new belief is

....

....

7. And I will show this by (be specific: actions, words, phrases, etc.)

....

....

fuck #5

Be Stifled

"*The deepest pain I ever felt was denying my own feelings to make everyone else comfortable.*"

—NICOLE LYONS

Ah, emotions.

Women and men have (generally) differed in this area since the beginning of humanity. But things have changed.

It's time we stop giving into the fuck that to be taken seriously, a woman has to sterilize herself into an emotionless, one-dimensional robot or "act like a man." At the same time, we would also do well to stop calling little boys "pussies" or "girls" when they cry and publicly shaming and reducing a man who wants to spend time with his partner and children.

To have emotions is human, period.

This fuck is close to my heart, as you will see. I have had to *learn* over the course of two years to feel, to respect my feelings, and to see them as worthy. The words of my psychology professor have frequently resounded in my head:

"Feelings just *are*."

Women are taught that our own, natural emotions are irrelevant, disruptive, crazy, irritating, or otherwise something to be suppressed, especially when dealing with our male counterparts, instead of a signal that something needs attention. If we start to feel dizzy when exercising, we change our behavior. We stop and sit down, or we might communicate how we are feeling to someone nearby. When we get cold, we grab a blanket. When we are hungry, we grab a brown—er, salad.

And when we are sad, angry, confused, proud, irritated, or feeling like we could take over the world, we apologize for it, dismiss it away, or minimize it. *Why?* For those of you running on fumes from a day of kids, work, and the typical mental load, the answer is: *someone else's fuck.*

My personal favorite is "crazy."

Admittedly, I used to buy into this fuck and call women crazy too. But eventually, I came to realize that some people who used this word typically deserved what they got. As I entered my thirties and dated a little more wisely (kind of), I would listen for my dates to refer to their "crazy" exes. This told me two things: the man lacked the type of vocabulary and maturity level I'm attracted to, and he was likely behaving illogically, gaslighting, cheating, or otherwise driving these women to act in a confused and frustrated manner (previously known as "crazy").

Female intuition is real. This is our superpower. Why else would it be threatening to the point of requiring gaslighting to combat it? We need to start teaching women and young girls that *they can listen to and trust their feelings* instead of apologizing for them or allowing them to be discounted, manipulated, or gaslighted into an oblivion of self-doubt.

Why would you want to water yourself down when there are so many interesting emotions to experience, leverage, and enjoy? Personally, I find people without a healthy emotional range to be a bore. Not only do emotions allow us to live a deeper, more colorful life; they are signals we can use to interpret and judge a situation—that is, if we can drop the fuck that sells us the story that emotions are silly, useless, or otherwise invaluable.

Research from the corporate world has found that female emotion can be extremely useful in making decisions. Daniel Kahneman suggests that in decision-making, logic only gets us so far, and then we benefit from our intuitive abilities. Emotional intelligence is consistently regarded as one of the top leadership skills. So why are we letting this belief drag us down?

The origin of this, at least in modern times, is clear. According to a few research studies, prior to around age five, boys and girls do not typically differentiate gender and the expectations that come with it. Then, little girls are given dolls and taught to be nurturing. Little boys are given G.I. Joes and told to be brave or walk it off when they are in emotional or physical pain. When girls reach adolescence, they've lost much of their confidence as they witness "girl" become a pejorative term. Crying is "for girls." Pink is "for girls." Also, it is a bad thing to be "like a girl."

A brilliant Always commercial highlighted this when they asked young girls to run, throw, and do other things "like a girl." They kicked ass and held back nothing. Then, they asked teen and adult women to do the same. Women demonstrated a run reminiscent of Seinfeld's character Elaine dancing spastically. The teens and adult women purposely diminished their own physical skills to portray a less coordinated, weaker, gendered version, even though they themselves were more capable.

Boys are also handed a gendered story about emotions from a young age, so it's not surprising that without someone to "right the ship" and teach them about the value of emotions, they may grow up to be men who have an extremely difficult time with emotional content (at best) or who become aggressive or violent due to their lack of appropriate coping skills, communication, and emotional displays like crying or seeking out support systems.

My heart has broken for some male clients when we get to exploring this topic. Even "That sounds very unfair. I'm sorry that happened to you," can bring tears to their eyes. Watching them struggle and become fearful when the floodgates reach capacity is a sensitive matter to be handled with support and care beyond anything I've ever had to offer female clients, who are generally more prepared and familiar with how their bodies and minds feel during emotional times.

Any woman who has been in a deep relationship with a man has likely experienced the turning point in which a man will open his emotional flood gates. There is *a lot* there, and women are adept at catching it all. Maybe you're familiar with this experience, or maybe you've seen this happen in every relationship you've ever been in. Maybe you eventually left a relationship because, while the floodgates were harboring dangerous levels of water, they just wouldn't open. Intuitive women know this emotional harboring is more dangerous than the moment the floodgates break open.

Besides with a wife, significant other, or their mother, men are not typically given spaces to discuss and work through highly emotional topics. Because men are humans and many humans reject what they fear or don't understand, men become adults who may see emotion as disruptive, confusing, inconvenient, or easily dismissible rather than a giant, critical piece of human development. Then, they drop this fuck on the women in their lives—partners, siblings, and coworkers alike. It stifles interpersonal and intrapersonal communication, creating a rift between loved ones that lasts until a shitload of work is done among all involved parties.

Amy Schumer regales us with the repercussions of this unfortunate childhood phenomenon in her hilarious standup performance *Amy Schumer: Growing*. Grown adults tell little girls, "He pulled your hair and pushed you on the playground? He must like you!" In that moment, we excuse the behavior. We also diminish the girl's feelings about it, as she is likely to be confused or upset (read: *You're mistaken for feeling that way, a.k.a. Fuck #3*). And we put that kind of behavior on a pedestal as an actual form of romantic communication instead of a more safe, appropriate, "Hi! I like you."

Why, then, are we surprised when little girls grow up to understand abusive, rude, or otherwise inappropriate behavior as flirty, strong, or manly? Why are we surprised that women hang in there, in the name of "love" and through all the red flags, with the hope that their partner will one day truly care for them as they want and need to be cared for? What kind of a world would we live in if we stopped teaching girls and women that men "just aren't emotional" or "just don't know any better" and started teaching boys and men about emotions?

One particularly tough evening, I went to spend the night with my friends Stephanie and Bill (we have "puppy sleepovers" that just warm my soul). They cooked me amazing Cambodian food, and we drank wine from our favorite Santa Ynez vineyard and talked under bistro lights outside. I was craving emotional depth and the opportunity to connect through vulnerability. I had become increasingly sick of denying that need within my marriage, and I was thankful to have like-valued friends with whom to share my thoughts.

Stephanie and I began discussing how freeing it was to experience the emotional range we have as women. We embraced it in that moment while Bill, her husband, fell silent.

Eventually, he spoke up and said, with his head down, "As a male, that is really hard to do around most people." Stephanie and I listened as Bill shed light on how for males, emotional depth and vulnerability are punished. "It's very much still seen as 'a female thing' and ridiculed within male friend groups," he explained. I felt a wave of gratitude for that moment. We were sharing a very real human injustice, and the three of us continued to bond over how showing emotion as a male earned insults like "pussy" or "pushover" and how, as females, being emotional earned us titles like "bitch," "crazy," or "dramatic."

I closed my eyes and let the wine set in, imagining a world where men and women having conversations like this was the norm instead of the unrequited desire of women everywhere. Imagine what music, art, and other creative fields would be like without the gift of dynamic and deep *feels*! Everyone deserves to live in a world where they are free to experience a healthy emotional range. Emotions are not an annoying inconvenience; they are normal reactions to our environment that provide valuable signals for our behavior.

Plus, who doesn't love a good cry?

Years after my parents got divorced, I got kicked out of my mother's house (a whole other book) and went to live with my father. Given that he was significantly older than most of my friends' fathers, he lacked the energy and wherewithal to control his stubborn teenage daughter. This led to a few fun years of our house being "the party house."

During one particular party, my father pulled one of my friends aside and asked about me: "Why is she so *angry*?"

"She's not angry," my friend told him. "She's passionate."

The next day my father told me what he'd learned. After years of telling me "Don't get hyper," he sounded relieved to have a "passionate" daughter and not an "angry" one.

Several years later, while I was in college and clearly experiencing depression, he wrote in a letter, "You're not as unique as you think you are. Everyone else has your problems too." Essentially, he was telling me, "Suck it up." It took me a few more years to put together that he was giving me this fuck based on his own feelings about depression—a fuck passed to him by his father.

Fucks from the fam. How many are you racking up?

I'm happy to report that when I was in graduate school, my father traveled to visit me in DC. Over Asian fusion, he asked me to explain what happens in a depressed and anxious brain. He was interested and ready to see his experience from a different perspective. When I was a kid, he would drive two towns over to see his psychologist because he was so embarrassed about his feelings and subsequent lack of control over them.

A company president I used to coach said to me, "Sometimes I just wish it was okay to cry." When I asked, "Why isn't it okay?" he looked at me blankly and with a bit of surprise, as if he'd never even questioned this belief before.

It's difficult to face what we don't understand or what we have been told is wrong. Although this book is about how women are conditioned throughout life, men are no different. They were raised in environments where their emotions were likely treated as inconvenient, dismissible, or devalued, instead of signals that something (or someone) needed attention. If we societally pair "crying" with "like a girl" and "like a girl" with "less than," we create adult males who have no idea what to do when they want to cry and women who reserve their tears for the silent confines of office bathrooms, home closets, or their commute home. They hide it or, more often, hold it back, because feelings are silly, inconvenient, and ambiguous. They rarely truly get to experience the luxury of emotional range and the shared connection that comes with "showing your human" to another person.

When I consider where much of the hurtful, harmful, or down-right intolerable male behavior comes from, I find there is nearly always a story that helps me understand (or, as we analysts would say, "identify the consequences that maintain the behavior"). I know better than most that behavior always comes from somewhere. I've seen many men struggle with their own vulnerabilities and injustices, including in my work with Navy SEALs when breaking down who they are so they can happily and authentically transition into a new world of civilian life. I would dare go so far as to say that men are more sensitive and vulnerable than women.

That being said, *explaining* and *understanding* behavior is far different than accepting it, excusing it, or adding it to our list of fucks, especially when it harms us in the process.

The idea that being taken seriously as a woman means turning into a lifeless, stoic robot without sadness, excitement, concern, or joy is not only something that needs changing; it is shown to kill innovation and deflate work relationships. If you haven't noticed, it is also a very tacky '90s corporate version of professional. If women are clawing their way to the C-suite, then we have the opportunity to stop being so outdated. Go ahead. Pepper your emails with exclamation marks and smiley faces if you're feeling it.

To the leaders reading this right now, you officially have permission to bring your emotions to work—if not for you, then for the women (and everyone else) around you who secretly want to do the same. If not for them, then for the young ladies behind you, watching and learning what a leader looks like. Talk about your fears and concerns while avoiding toxic optimism and positivity, which immediately brushes the issue and the feelings that follow under the rug. Create psychological safety in your organization by leading with your human side. Rebuild your post-pandemic culture as one that genuinely invites and encourages warmth, compassion, and connection through feeling along with doing.

You—you beautiful, interesting being—have the luxury of experiencing the wide emotional range that adds zest to your life, depth to your relationships, and a profound intuition that deserves to be honed as a skill instead of squashed as a bother or weakness. You can move freely in your emotions, giving permission to everyone around you.

It's time we stop giving into the fuck that to be taken seriously women have to sterilize themselves into something one-dimensional. As a social media post I saw recently so brilliantly stated:

I asked my kid what their favorite color was.

My kid: Gold with glitter in it.

Me: Glitter isn't a color.

My kid: It's a lifestyle.

If your eyes are welling up just thinking about how much you hold back on a daily basis, this could be the fuck for you.

*My emotional
range is my
superpower.
I greet each
feeling with a
warm embrace.*

Fuck Being
Stifled

Consider with curiosity:

- When and with whom must you stifle your emotions?
- When and with whom do you enjoy showing a wide emotional range?
- Where did your story of being emotionally sterile come from?
- What is maintaining it, and what are you getting from it?
- What is likely to happen if you keep this fuck?

YOUR REWRITE

In the following exercise, fill in the blanks when you feel inspired and clear. You can choose to commit to these new beliefs any time you're ready.

1. I'm dropping the belief that

....

....

2. Because

....

....

3. If I'm successful, (what will happen?)

....

....

4. If I'm successful, I will have time and energy for

....

....

5. And it will feel

....

....

6. My new belief is

....

....

7. And I will show this by (be specific: actions, words, phrases, etc.)

....

....

Be Everything

"Saddest of all are the women who were brought up to believe that self-sacrifice is the highest female virtue. They made the sacrifice, often willingly, and they are still waiting for the blessing."

—JEANETTE ANNE DIMECH

Remember the poem by Lily Myers? Have you been considering where these fucks have been coming from in your own life?

Here's a familial scene:

For my entire childhood, I watched the women in my family spend hours in the kitchen, intermittently serving the men beer, snacks, and, eventually, a full meal while they watched the "big game" on Thanksgiving and Christmas. Then I watched all the women take the men's plates and clean up the mess left behind. I can't remember one instance where the men offered to help, and I can't remember one instance where they were asked to.

When we are asked to manage many things at once at work, we are called project managers. It's an entire job that comes with a salary, benefits, and vacation time, not to mention promotions and social connections with coworkers. However, when women carry out this job in the home, even if they have another job at an office, we call it…well, we call it "being a woman." Studies show that even women who outearn their husbands still accept around 60–80 percent of the mental load of their households.

A few years ago, I wrote a blog titled "Why I'm Never Busy." It was my way of coming out of the self-aggrandizing closet of martyrdom I'd built for myself. Instead of telling people how "busy" I was, I resolved to wipe the word from my vocabulary completely. I was no longer a crazy-busy woman punctuating her sentences with exasperated sighs to alert everyone to how important and needed she was, hoping for a, "Wow, you really do it all!" or some similar verbal accolade.

Knowing that any behavior you are trying to reduce or eliminate requires a functionally equivalent replacement behavior (see appendix), I decided to frame my life with a *new* word. What would I say when people asked me how I was doing or what I was up to? I thought a lot about my replacement word. I could just fake a smile and say, "Everything is great!" But feigning emotions hasn't ever been my style. I'm terrible at it. I could redirect people back to themselves, but then I'd never get to talk about my own life and what I was actually up to. Finally, I landed on the word that would from then on describe my life—a word that changed my own narrative.

From that point on, I would look at my life not as busy, but *fulfilling.*

This not only changed my perspective toward one of gratitude, but it made me realize that everything I was taking on in my life was my choice. I chose to work a few jobs and take on extra projects. I chose a relationship. I chose travel. I chose to host dinner parties for my friends. No one cared how "busy" I was (because cry me a river—they're all busy too), and once I fully recognized the social currency of "busy," my martyrdom felt tacky and commonplace.

I was now "fulfilled," which felt pretty fucking good.

Going from busy and overworked to living a life of fulfilling activities required eliminating "busy" from my vocabulary, and it also changed my conversations with others.

My interactions went from something like this:

"How are you?"

"Ugh, I'm *so* busy! I've got an article due, and oh, I decided to start a book with my colleagues and…"

"Ugh, I know! I've got the kids and this dinner party I'm hosting and…"

(Yada-yada, same old conversation. *Boring.*)

To this:

"How are you?"

"I'm feeling more fulfilled. I'm loving the writing process, and I'm almost done with that article…"

"So great! I'm hosting that dinner party this weekend and I'm learning to make a new appetizer…"

NOTE

I actually do *love* writing, it's a fire of mine. I can't say whether or not my friends actually loved what they were discussing in response. There is a big difference between *forcing* positivity about something you don't give a fuck about and *reframing* something you're passionate about as an act of gratitude and energy preservation.

My entire way of relating to the world changed, and it changed the people that I kept around me. To be fair, there were still the garden variety conversations of kids, work, and life stress but, in comparison, I could feel how they depleted me. The friends that jumped on my "life is *fulfilling*" train energized me, and I learned so much more about what things they were taking on and learning about.

It felt positive; I was in charge. I also received an unexpected bonus—I noticed that many of the things taking my time weren't *actually* fulfilling. This made it easier to ask myself, "Then what *am* I getting out of this?" Once I went from "busy" (mostly made up of tasks other people expected of me) to "fulfilled" (activities and projects that truly gave me energy and purpose), so much changed. I didn't love everything in my life, but I loved a hell of a lot more.

It's empowering to feel the ways in which changing our language can lead to such unintended, powerful consequences. The words we use to communicate with ourselves and others frame the movie of our lives every day, and it can be harmful and depleting to direct your movie with a shitty script. No one wants to watch that movie, let alone live it.

Maybe my particular example of replacing "busy" with "fulfilling" resonates with you. Maybe some other words are coming up. It's possible you'd like to eradicate "let" or "allow" from your vocabulary. For example, "My company won't *allow* us to take our whole vacation," or "My kids won't *let* me turn the TV off before they're ready." Whatever is coming up for you, write it down. Really sit and think about the way you speak to yourself and the world, because your words are powerful. They matter more than you think they do, and they deserve further consideration.

Among all the words we can change in order to get fuck-free, we will now focus on the most dangerous word in the English language. Hell, in any language.

It's not *can't*.

It's not won't.

It's not *no*.

It's not *hate*.

It's *but*.

I know I want this, *but*…

I know I should, *but*…

I know I would be fantastic at this, *but*…

I want to visit there, *but*…

I want that promotion, *but*…

I hate my job, *but*…

I want to improve my health, *but*…

I know I shouldn't take this anymore, *but*…

I know I'm meant to _____, *but*…

And the top "but" to explore in this chapter: I don't want to "do it all" anymore and it's crushing me, *but* if I don't do it, no one else will.

Using this word:

- creates mental and emotional barriers
- demeans your wants and needs
- lessens the possibility of meeting that specific want or need
- signals to others that your wants or needs are less important and thus up for compromise
- demotivates you
- puts you second, third, or fourth in your own life
- gives power to someone or something else

This particular word also makes wild assumptions.

What do I mean by that?

I mean that you're basing your behavior off of shit data. I mean that we also use "but" as an assumption that we already know what will happen if we try (in this case, to stop "doing it all" and see who jumps in to help), so we state the want or need out loud but then reel it back in out of fear that it won't go well. It's the equivalent of making a joke but really meaning it. But do we really mean it? Because now someone else has to expend energy working through what we might have meant, because we're too much of a weenie to just say it and give them the information they need. It's confusing, and it irritates people.

Or maybe that's just me.

"I want that promotion, but I don't think I'm qualified."

"I really like them, but I don't think they would be into me."

"I'm not happy in my marriage, but things aren't bad enough to leave."

"I don't think I want children, but my partner/parents would be devastated if I told them."

Let's call these what they are: more fucks. So what if you don't think you're qualified? So what if you think someone else will be upset? So what if you don't think that hottie is into you? Does it change what you truly want, or does this temporary doubt and nervousness just make that job, love interest, or lifestyle a little bit more fun to go after? In these moments you have two choices: continue to orbit and adjust around everyone else and remain comfortable, or embrace a moment of *Fuckless*ness and do it anyway for the simple reason that you want to.

Men are taught to be brave, have fun, and approach life with an adventurous conquistador attitude, knowing that they should go for what they want without regard for the consequences (for better or worse). Men around the world get brutally rejected all the time, and it turns out they're faring just fine. They don't have to carry the story that being rejected equals being wrong like women do. Some also have insane levels of unjustified confidence. And if they can, then you can too.

So, *fuck it*! Can you challenge yourself to drop the belief that you have to be everything to everyone first and, instead, see what happens when you take wild risks for your *own* life with the confidence of a drunk unicorn?

Here are some exercises to get you started:

- Apply for a job you're incredibly underqualified for but that you dream about.
- Chat up the hottest person you can find with the intention of walking away two minutes in.
- Sign up for a class on a subject you are far from understanding (try www.coursera.com).

You'll soon learn that tossing the "must be right and liked forever and always" narrative into the toilet opens doors, creates freedom, and feels pretty damn good.

So maybe you don't get the job or the love interest. So you spoke your truth about what you want for yourself and it angered or disappointed some people. It does not mean you are not liked or worthy or that your desires do not matter. It means that those are not your people.

I get it. Fear is *real*. Fear of rejection, fear of embarrassment, fear of being wrong. Fear of feeling, once again, like you're not good enough. Sometimes fear is just too much to face. I get that. There have been times in my life where being brave, even with something small, felt like it would break me if it didn't go well. If this is where you are, then put the book down. Now is not an optimal time for running into dark caves and burning buildings. And that is 100 percent okay. That is not failure; it's being smart about what you're ready for. And when you're ready to pick this book up again, you'll be better prepared to give your fucks away. I want this to be an exciting endeavor for you, not something that changes you by force. Just know that this process is scary either way, so it's important that you're prepared and positive.

We make so many assumptions about what will happen or what it will mean if we even occasionally choose ourselves instead of everyone else first. It breaks my heart to hear women add *more* barriers to their lives by accommodating and diminishing their wants and needs away.

This calls to my mind my favorite perspective-taking exercise. A few years ago, I read *The Monk Who Sold His Ferrari*. In it, Robin Sharma puts a name to the process by which I've learned to make decisions about how I live my life: "the deathbed mentality." Morbid? Sure. But humor me here.

Set a timer for five minutes, and close your eyes. Picture yourself on your deathbed. To make it less of a bummer, let's say you're very old and about to die peacefully surrounded by loved ones.

Look back at your life: your loved ones, your successes, your failures, your vacations, your hobbies, your work, everything.

From your deathbed, what do you wish you had done now that you fully understand the feeling of being on limited time? Write it down now. Write down all of your hidden desires, your unspoken truths, the things you would do if nobody was judging.

If that's too much, sit on your "deathbed" and repeat your buts:

"I wanted to see Dylan in concert, but I had that Tuesday meeting my boss needed me for."

"I wanted to go a year being single, but that sounded like a long time."

"I wanted to start a side business as an artist, but I just didn't have the time."

Hopefully deathbed you is shaking current you violently. You could've seen Dylan! You could've spent a year as something other than someone's wife or girlfriend! You could've become a career artist, or at least created art that fulfilled you and made you happy!

Consider the decision to drop this fuck and experience the thrill of feeling free of roles you just don't want to play anymore or tasks that crush your soul (looking at you, PTA mama who makes the classroom cookies from scratch, runs a business, cleans the house, and collapses in a heap at the end of the day). That thing that's popping into your mind? The wish that says, *If I didn't have to* ____ *anymore, I would have so much more energy.* Let that voice speak a little louder; see what she has to say.

And know this: *no one is judging what you give up anywhere near as much as you're judging yourself.* No one will ever hand you a medal for most sacrifices made, and it's a lonely race.

When we try to be everything, we always miss out on something. Don't let your buts become your could-haves.

"Not today, everyone."

No one needs me as much as I first need myself.

Fuck Being Everything

Consider with curiosity:

- When and with whom is being everything rewarded?
- When and with whom is drawing boundaries and creating space for yourself rewarded?
- How does it feel to create space to do exactly what serves you?
- Where did your story of being everything come from?
- What is maintaining it, and what are you getting from it?
- What is likely to happen if you keep this fuck?

This is a big one, so I've added these additional questions:

- While you're doing it all, do you enjoy it for the most part?
- What are you giving up in the process?
- Who are you doing it all for, and where did you get the idea that it's all on you? Is it true?

If you find yourself thinking, *I have so many fucks to drop here*, or *I'm being depleted by doing it all*, complete the following exercise specifically crafted for this fuck:

For the next few days, keep a list of all your "yeah, buts." All the things you want to make time for but don't because you're carrying such an enormous mental, emotional, or physical workload that could be shared. Challenge yourself to notice how often you use the word "but" then make assumptions based off of a shitty script or a false story (or an unfortunately true story). Think about how your mental load stops you from doing what makes you happy, even just for a few hours.

If you're feeling a little angry, try not to judge yourself. This is a hard one.

YOUR REWRITE

In the following exercise, fill in the blanks when you feel inspired and clear. You can choose to commit to these new beliefs any time you're ready.

1. I'm dropping the belief that

....

....

2. Because

....

....

3. If I'm successful, (what will happen?)

....

....

4. If I'm successful, I will have time and energy for

....

....

5. And it will feel

....

....

6. My new belief is

....

....

7. And I will show this by (be specific: actions, words, phrases, etc.)

....

....

fuck #7

Be Chosen

"A woman needs a man like a fish needs a bicycle."

—GLORIA STEINEM

Remember my aforementioned affinity for the F-word? It began at age ten.

One day after I dropped an F-bomb, my mother calmly said to me, "You know, honey, boys won't like you if you talk like that." Props to her for taking that approach, as I was entering middle school and most girls that age do start to notice boys. The problem was it had never occurred to me to care what boys thought of me. They were still more of a nuisance than a variable to my behavior. I had honestly found that swearing lent the perfect punctuation needed to get my point across and, most importantly, to make people notice me (like I said, I was always the runt).

More disruptive to her valiant effort to turn me into a child with acceptable social skills, soon after her warning, I got my first boyfriend. He took notice of me as we bonded over our potty mouths. True story. Whenever we would see each other in the halls, in a romantic call-and-response, one of us would say, "What's the greatest word in the world?" and the other would let out an elated, giggly, "Fuck!" While our young romance was short-lived, we are still friends to this day. He is my mother's trusted and talented financial advisor, and his late father was instrumental in me buying my first home.

When I was told that boys wouldn't like me if I used swear words, this immediately signaled to my young brain that boyfriends were a very valuable staple in life and that my behavior should reflect what they would find likable so I would be chosen. I never once remember receiving the message that I should go focus on myself and that whoever loved me for the truest, most authentic version of myself would be an exponentially better fit.

When I bought my first home, I was a single, thirty-two-year-old woman. Among the congratulations, I received several warnings that it would intimidate the men I was dating. I'm sorry to say that on a few dates, I refrained from sharing this information because I felt it would affect my chances of being chosen. It did not occur to me to think, *If that's a problem, they can fuck right off.*

In my twenties, I spent time with a man who I knew liked me but who also notified me that I "didn't really come off as girlfriend material." Weeks before he told me this, I received a call at one in the morning from the front desk of my building about a man who was asking for me. I went down to see who it was and found this same man, shirtless, drunk, sweaty, and so disruptive I had to hurry him upstairs to avoid the police (he slept on the floor and woke up next to an empty pizza box). Even when notified that I didn't "present as girlfriend material," I internalized it and thought about what I could do differently—about what was wrong with me—instead of considering whether he was presenting himself as *boyfriend material*. It brought up a theme I've loathed since I was a teenager: girls have to behave so they are chosen, and boys get to play, cause trouble, sleep around, and take risks because they do the choosing and thus do not have to think about being chosen.

My dating life followed this pattern for another decade before fully sinking in, and it only fully landed when I decided to be single for an extended period of time. I still cringe that this is true.

How often do you experience the scenarios below?

1. You overhear a man receiving dating advice from another man: "Don't tell her about your promotion. It might scare her off. And say you rent, not own."
2. You open a magazine to find it filled with articles titled "How You Know If You're a Good Husband" and "5 Ways to Attract the Perfect Woman."
3. You walk into a party and meet three happily single, career-focused women in their forties, and no one mentions this fact as if they're unicorns
4. Your male friends start spending large blocks of their free time talking about their dates, getting ready for their dates, worrying about what their dates will think, and beating themselves up for saying that one thing that probably is the reason she didn't call afterward.
5. A man says, "No, I'm not seeing anyone right now. I'm too

busy with travel and work," and the other party says, "Don't worry. You'll find her when you're not looking! She's out there!" in a tone that suggests what he is currently doing with his life is secondary, filling time until a romantic interest comes along.

As I was considering the above myself, a line of several horrifying questions followed:

How much time and effort do women spend preparing for a girlfriend/wife role compared to the amount of time men spend preparing to be boyfriends/husbands?

(Starts sweating)

What if women spent the same amount of time (very little) preparing to be chosen—focusing on their wrinkles, dating, worrying about men, picking out outfits, self-loathing, dieting, searching dating apps, venting to friends, spending time in the wrong relationships, etc.—as men do?

(Heart pounds)

What if they took all that time and redirected it into their careers, traveling, friendships, or literally *anything* else?

(Anxiety attack ensues)

When I asked myself these questions, my heart broke. I wanted to cry—for myself and for the world that so desperately needs women's time, talent, and attention. To solve big problems. To fulfill their purposes. To speak their desires into existence. To live out loud with their ideas, energy, and passion without spending unbalanced amounts of time preparing to be chosen.

All these questions and words might be triggering for you. You might be thinking, *I don't spend all my time thinking about men! I don't prepare to be chosen!*

Fair enough. In no way am I assuming every woman out there experiences this. Each of the fucks in this book *may or may not* be true for you. I simply ask that you consider the extent to which you share these experiences or beliefs. If you'd told me two years ago that I would be having OSMs left and right about being chosen and orbiting around yet-to-exist boyfriends, I would've laughed in your face. Yet here we are.

The funny thing about humans is we tend to overestimate and underestimate our behavior depending on how positive or negative we think it is. For example, we may overestimate the number of times we've cleaned up after someone (exactly one million) but underestimate the amount of time we've yelled at our partner (like, *once* in twelve years). I used to tell myself I didn't have time to do the dishes. When I timed myself, it took me four minutes. It became easier (though not more enjoyable) to do the dishes because I proved my false belief wrong.

So humor me here and consider that you may be underestimating the time and energy you dedicate to thinking about or preparing to be chosen, even if it's triggering (especially if it's triggering). You bought this book to bravely challenge beliefs, and some stories become so normal for us that they become our (false) reality.

According to The Bechdel Test Fest, the Bechdel test, also

known as the Bechdel–Wallace test, in the movie industry is "a basic measure to see if women are fairly represented in a film." A film only passes the Bechdel Test if it has two female characters who have names that talk to each other about something other than a man.

You might be thinking, *That's ridiculous. Plenty of movies include two women who talk about something other than a man.*

In 2016, about 50 percent of the twenty-five highest-grossing movies passed this test.

Yeah. Let that sink in.

Now ask yourself how many conversations in your own life would pass the test.

Again, this isn't to shit on romantic relationships, marriage, men, or dish sessions on your dating life. It's to consciously take a beat, question without judgment, and decide whether there is an opportunity to recalibrate so you can move toward a truer, more beautiful version of you.

I broke up with a boyfriend six months after we moved to California and, even though I knew almost no one, I felt that familiar sense of freedom and positivity I had always felt after leaving relationships. I started to realize that maybe it *was* me. After six serious relationships, I started to entertain the idea that maybe I would never be able to be the fullest expression of myself while I was part of a twosome. I also saw a depressing pattern. Not only did I love being single, but I also left for the same reason every time: I felt like I could no longer grow within the confines of that relationship. I felt boxed in and responsible to continue to be the same woman I was when the relationship started. Then I looked back on twenty years of side comments and intimidation from boyfriends regarding my vocabulary, finances, intellect, and desired lifestyle. I realized I *was* boxed in. Not only could I not be fully actualized in the context of my own relationships, but I had shrunk myself—mind, body, and soul—beyond recognition to accommodate the partnership.

If you're thinking, *She must be seriously bad at choosing partners*, please know this: with the exception of two men, I can comfortably say that every other person with whom I've had a relationship has been very kind, well-intended, and lovely. I'm still friends with many exes and have even attended their weddings (and invited them to mine). But in the end, I still allowed myself to overaccommodate, be small, and the like, because that's the story I first received and sold myself for years.

And that was on me.

When I decided to take a few years to be single, it seemed like a crazy idea. But when I reviewed the previous decade and realized I'd only been single for a total of eleven months, I knew this was one of the seemingly crazy, definitely uncomfortable shifts I wanted to make. So I decided to be single for a year. I was shocked at how much I enjoyed it, and I decided to continue this path for as long as it served me. It was difficult at times, but I knew I was recalibrating a part of my consciousness and lifestyle that would result in improving my life and reclaiming space I previously reserved for romantic partnerships. If and when I chose to have a partner in the future, the relationship would be that much healthier and fulfilling.

And sure enough, something big happened as a result.

I realized that I was holding space for a person who didn't yet exist in my life. I'd have thoughts like, *I hope whoever I end up with wants to live in Europe one day too*, as if I'd never get to fulfill that dream if they didn't. As if there would definitely be a "them" around in the first place. I was already in orbit around whoever would come into my life in the future, hedging my big life moves—like where I would buy my next home—until my next relationship. I knew I could overcome this by not only taking a break from dating, but by removing the assumption I'd have a permanent partner at all. I would just live and love for myself.

Once I removed the assumption that I'd have a partner to travel with, to live with, to fix stuff, to sleep with, and to take into consideration, I got to experience what life as a man must be like. My life became about *me*. The decisions I made, the career moves I chose, the fact that I wrote this book are largely because I stopped waiting on what my next relationship would bring and who I would adjust myself around. I saw a hesitation and a waiting that shocked me. And without it, there was so much more time and energy to focus on exactly what I wanted:

- fulfilling my dream of being an author
- growing my businesses and having time for meeting bright, talented people
- healing and growing beyond what I thought was possible
- taking classes and learning about things that interest me
- buying a gorgeous and serene 1931 vintage cottage three thousand miles from my current city
- becoming more familiar with my body, my orgasms, and my sexual identity

- learning how to understand and run my own finances

It wasn't that I didn't want a partner ever again—I very much love being in (good) relationships. It was that I was truly enjoying the experience of living as though I was enough instead of buying into the belief that because I didn't have a partner, there was something off-putting, wrong, or unattractive about me. It took some time to get used to, as all habits do, but I wouldn't give this time (which is still in process) up for anything.

I'll admit this came after being married, divorced, and receiving an inheritance from my father's passing. There were variables to this lifestyle that made it easier for me than for someone who very much wants a partner and a family or who does not have financial independence. Financial means is often a big determinant for women making choices on whether to enter or leave a relationship. I can remember wanting to leave my relationship when I lived in Washington, DC, but I couldn't yet afford to live alone. I want to honor this as a societal struggle related to education, domestic abuse, pay gaps, city life, and opportunities for women that are nowhere near equal to men.

That being said, this next part is for the women who have the option to choose and who are in the position to evaluate whether they want a partner, when, and why.

Years ago, during one of my regular visits to Manhattan, my friends and I were enjoying a good old-fashioned girls night. One of them—let's call her Naomi—was venting about the NYC dating scene. "I haven't met anyone I've clicked with! I go to all these sports bars…" she said. Naomi didn't do sports. Not even a little bit. What she *did* end up doing was spending weekends in smelly bars standing on peanut shells while competing with Tom Brady for the attention of the men around her. We were all perplexed.

The extent to which we want a partner makes us more or less likely to develop fucks that can completely derail who we are or want to be. The deprivation and satiation of romantic involvement or options also weighs heavily here. Assuming we want a relationship or at least carry the fuck that we do, that can look something like this (more on this in the appendix):

- deprivation of romantic partnership = increases value of romantic partnership
- satiation of romantic partnership (lots of options, messaging on dating apps, just out of a long relationship, etc.) = decreases the value of a romantic partnership

In plain terms, if we put a high value on something (or someone), we are more likely to compromise ourselves and our needs and wants in exchange for the partner or partnership. We may also turn a blind eye and excuse away all those red flags (it is not a carnival—walk away now). This is when we *look* like we give a fuck about something—we even *think* we give a fuck about something—but after time we realize that we've compromised ourselves into a tricky spot. We begin to feel the weight of spending huge blocks of time doing things that don't actually align with who we are and what we want in a partner. Maybe you've said you've wanted big, important things you really don't in order to remain agreeable and chosen. Maybe you've become a less authentic version of yourself in order to be a better fit, increasing the likelihood the relationship will be successful.

Only you know what you've compromised and if you feel a loss. But what would it be like to be loved and chosen *because* of those things you've tossed aside, those interests or personality traits, or desires?

As Esther Perel says of relationships: "Eroticism thrives in the space between the self and the other."

A friend of mine dated a married man for five years. They fell hard for each other in the first years of his marriage to another woman. At first, he had a six-month plan to leave his wife. Then it became a year. Year after year, she stuck by him as he canceled trips she had paid for, as he had a child, and as more years of her life were spent waiting. At one point, she asked me if I thought he would ever fulfill the promises he made her.

It had become about her being chosen. Despite the clear messaging, she didn't want to lose or give up those years of emotional labor. Understandable.

This is called the *sunk cost fallacy*. Christopher Olivola, an assistant professor of marketing at Carnegie Mellon, defined this in a *Time* article:

> The sunk cost is the general tendency for people to continue an endeavor, or continue consuming or pursuing an option, if they've invested time or money or some resource in it.

The sunk cost fallacy occurs when we continue to put effort into a person or project simply because we've *already* put so much time and effort in. We don't want to give up, so we continue trying to make a broken or wrong thing work. The shitty thing is, we incur an *opportunity cost*, which is all the time we give up and the things we say no to in the process. Essentially, we emotionally dig our heels in instead of logically stepping back and taking a more objective perspective.

I asked my friend to write down the things he did, said, and stood for, and I told her to look at the list and consider if those were things she wanted in a partner. She pushed the question and asked, from a behavioral perspective, if he would leave his wife. I said that people typically do not make choices on their own after this much time unless they experience consequences, and I suggested she try walking away.

The relationship took two more years of her life and never worked out. The allure of being chosen is extremely seductive and cloudy when you're in it.

Another friend of mine met a man a few weeks after his wedding. They talked for weeks and saw each other a few times over the summer. She was genuinely torn apart by her love for a married man, but after a few months, she decided to walk away. He was torn apart as well, and left his marriage after several months. While they were riddled with grief for how things started, they are now happily married and starting a family.

Shit happens. People fall in and out of love, and life is messy. This isn't about judgment. It is about the benefit women can gain from feeling genuinely enough instead of buying into the fact that we must be chosen to be validated in our existence and worthy. We can choose our own circumstances regarding who we date, marry, and sleep with and what we tolerate from those individuals. Period.

When women believe they are enough:

- They attract people who more naturally fit who they are and what they want in life.
- They are more likely to walk away from something that doesn't suit them.
- They are more likely to approach people of interest instead of waiting and giving them all the power.
- They can recover more quickly when feelings are not reciprocal.
- They are less likely to compromise themselves past recognition.
- They invest more time in themselves, for themselves.
- They naturally command respect because they signal that they have it for themselves.

This is not to say that making compromises in relationships is a bad thing. You know that's not true. But compromises can be normal and healthy or hurtful and damaging. Only you know which are which. If your mind is filling up with examples of ways you've changed beyond your recognition, then the relationship, or how you show up in it, may be dragging you down, consuming too much energy, or just not authentic to who you are. And that's okay too. Now you know.

Another thing I will ask you to consider are the stories you have about romantic relationships.

What do you believe or hope a romantic relationship will provide for you?

What might it take away or disrupt?

Why is now a good or bad time for a relationship?

Looking back, have you waited to be chosen without asking yourself if *you* would choose *them*?

If you choose to have a partner, get clear on yourself first, without the influence of anyone else. Wanting the same things is important. This is your *life*. Do you really want to spend it doing things you don't care about? More importantly, having a partner who shares your interests is pure magic. Remember *your* interests? They are just as valuable as what your crush likes to do with their time (I know it's weird, but believe it).

Regardless of whether this fuck resonates with you, this belief affects us all. Many women have been given the message—through entertainment, generational messages, and even political events—that their societal role and value is as wives or girlfriends, so *the value of romantic partners increases*. This creates competition among us. It angers me deeply because it distracts women from the magic of being collaborative and viewing themselves as powerful forces together. Instead, we are reduced to competing for the attention of potential partners. Do men compete for partners as well? Sure. But because their roles in society are more heavily predicated on money and career success, we have not seen as much societal competition among men for romantic relationships.

The gorgeous badass who (unknowingly and without malicious intent) intimidates you at work or in the school pickup line was not born that way; she changed some things and rose up over and over again to become who she is right now. She was born with everything you were: sexism, unrealistic beauty standards, and gender bias in the workplace (and everywhere). You are her; she is you.

The main difference is that she stopped taking on everyone else's fucks, focused on herself, and invested in unapologetically meeting her own wants and needs. And it was probably really fucking terrible and really fucking hard. And it probably took a really long time. She probably lost some friends. Maybe it led to a divorce. And she probably has battle scars you'll never see unless you ask.

Go talk to her. Ask her about her story. Stop looking at her and comparing yourself to her. That's your learning history of other people's fucks telling you that women are competition and that she's probably a bitch because she's attractive, confident, and smart. You're better than that. Drop those fucks and go be her friend. She has the "I peed my pants at a kegger in college" stories just like you do (and if you need other tragically embarrassing stories that make you feel like less of a loser, call me).

A popular saying in behavior analysis is that "behavior goes where reinforcement flows." If we value and reward men based upon their career success and money and reward women on their ability to obtain romantic relationships and have children, that expectation is what we will generally continue to fulfill. Then that narrative will continue to be perpetuated. Men do crazy things for power and money, and women waste time competing to be chosen. To me, this is an unfortunate fuck to give anyone. It's a distraction that takes away from friendships, growth, work, and genuine connection among and within all genders.

We would do better for those around us if we encouraged and supported people as *individuals* according to their own desires instead of continuing to reward specific genders based on tired narratives of what gives someone value.

If this fuck resonates with you, spend some time with the questions below before moving on to the exercise on the next page.

- Do you want a partner at this time in your life? For what reasons?
- What have you compromised in relationships that you wish you could finally be appreciated for?
- Has loneliness or financial challenges affected the value you put on having a partner?
- Do you feel pressured by family or society to have a partner?
- Do you hold the belief that your life cannot be successful or complete unless you have a romantic relationship?
- Can you embrace your unique self with the partner you currently have, or do you find yourself constantly maneuvering?
- Think about your favorite, healthiest relationship. What was the one component that made it so?

I am more interested in choosing than in being chosen.

Fuck Being Chosen

Consider with curiosity:

- When and with whom do you feel pressured to have a partner?
- When and with whom is choosing yourself or deciding to be single rewarded?
- Where did your story of being chosen come from?
- What is maintaining it, and what are you getting from it?
- What is likely to happen if you keep this fuck?

YOUR REWRITE

In the following exercise, fill in the blanks when you feel inspired and clear. You can choose to commit to these new beliefs any time you're ready.

1. I'm dropping the belief that

....

....

2. Because

....

....

3. If I'm successful, (what will happen?)

....

....

4. If I'm successful, I will have time and energy for

....

....

5. And it will feel

....

....

6. My new belief is

....

....

7. And I will show this by (be specific: actions, words, phrases, etc.)

....

....

fuck #8

Be Dependent

"*And where should a lady go on her travels? The world has hardly been her oyster in the past, thanks to the old chivalric image of the gentler, fairer, weaker sex....Assuming she is the sort of person willing to go abroad without some champion to protect her, she is still hardly equipped with the constitution to endure epic desert treks or polar crossings, to conquer really respectable mountains, or hole herself up with some secret tropic tribe somewhere.*"

—*UNSUITABLE FOR LADIES: AN ANTHOLOGY OF WOMEN TRAVELLERS*

Women receive signals that they should depend on a man for a variety of things. In this chapter, we will explore the two nearest and dearest to my heart (and experience): travel and entrepreneurship.

I found myself sitting in an LA boardroom interviewing for a lateral move within my company. They needed people to help out in their San Francisco office, and since I love to save sinking things, I threw my hat in the ring. The job was exactly the same job I'd been doing for years, but I would instead be taking a one-hour flight up to the Bay Area twice a month to work for the day, stay overnight, work the next day, and then come home.

I always interview well, and I was completely prepared, save for one question.

The man interviewing me, now known forever in my mind as Rick the Dick, asked about how I would deal with the inconvenience of travel and mansplained that traveling for work "isn't as glamorous as you'd think." I internally smirked at this remark, understanding that it likely came from someone who'd never left the state, and began to prove my ability to withstand an hourlong flight by listing some of my travel experiences:

- I spent a month backpacking through Southeast Asia with a girlfriend.
- I flew to Greece and back (all by myself!).
- I traversed through forty-two countries.
- I attended the Men's World Cup in Rio and drove through Chile a bit, navigating a hairy situation with military men and machine guns on a road trip gone wrong.
- I drove across the country twice (also by myself!).

To officially drop the mic and win the day, I threw in that I'd be going to Cambodia and Thailand (a second time) for my honeymoon.

"Oh. So what effect do you think that will have on your ability to do this job?" he asked.

At first I was confused as to why being married would matter. I was shocked silent while my brain searched for an answer. I'm sorry to say that all I could muster at the time was, "You mean, getting married? Um…my husband would be okay with it, if that's what you're asking."

It took another hour for my brain to process what had happened, and while I was driving home, I finally formed the words.

That question never would have been asked of a man.

Then another injustice entered my thoughts:

I went too far. He was threatened.

I was enraged. Tears of frustration poured down my face as I drove past Camp Pendleton. The Pacific Ocean that had once promised me potential and opportunity now seemed dull. I drove right to the bar and ordered a giant beer for lunch. I felt so defeated. I'd spent my entire life getting educated, being independent, and making huge decisions like leaving a relationship and going alone to a new city so I would grow to be a woman who had opportunities she wasn't scared to take. I'd built myself this lifestyle and forced myself to do things that were scary, like traveling the world, so I would never have to sit across from some prick who still treated me like I was the incapable one.

As someone who has traveled the streets of Manhattan, Los Angeles, Ensenada, Siem Reap, Berlin, Rio de Janeiro, Paris, Bangkok, Koh Kut, Vienna, Vang Vieng, Santiago, Marbella, Stockholm, and Lisbon, to name a few, I can tell you that *any* woman who is willing and able can do the same. It's important to reiterate that being "financially independent" has a lot to do with the freedom to travel, but traveling the world does not have to be expensive. There are numerous resources to travel economically, which I highly suggest looking into. Adventurous does not always equal expensive; my room in Thailand was six dollars per night!

I've been careful not to judge your beliefs thus far. If your definition of female is to be small, that is 100 percent your choice. If you believe your life will only be worthwhile if you have a partner, great! If you want to be the woman who does it all and puts everyone else first, get after that life. None of that is anyone's business but your own. This playbook simply gives you space to consider each belief as true or untrue for you and drop the ones that fail to serve the life you want.

However, my experience with travel is too personal for me not to gently add that if the belief that it is too dangerous, inconvenient, unfulfilling, or hard is keeping you from seeing the world, don't let it.

While traveling, I have:

- overcome a phase of crushing anxiety and become strong enough to end a stifling relationship and pursue graduate school
- had my only one-night stand with a man thirteen years my junior at the summit of a Greek island
- made incredible, interesting friends from all over the world
- visited Angkor Wat on the solstice sunrise
- been nearly brought to tears in countless museums, including the Louvre, Musée d'Orangerie, the Holocaust Museum

in Berlin, and the harrowing Museum of Memory and Human Rights in Santiago

- woken at sunrise for dozens of solo, exploratory city runs
- hot-tubbed in an old barrel and stargazed at the foot of the Alps, surrounded by pigs and chickens
- sat in the cook's quarters of a rural Chilean restaurant while the staff watched their country defeat Spain in the World Cup (a very, very big deal)
- learned to adore the feeling of being fully naked in public, receiving the gift of giggly, exhilarating joy in the process
- connected with people whose language I did not speak via charades and fits of laughter
- photographed an abandoned spy tower built atop a mountain of war rubble
- experienced the pre-pavement ride from Cambodia to Thailand, a combination of the game "chicken" and rally racing, with guns
- eaten a solo meal at L'Arpège in Paris and taken selfies with famed chef Alain Passard (his idea)
- danced in Brazilian clubs until my muscles burned and I was covered in sweat
- feasted on street snake, which is exactly what it sounds like
- taken cooking classes in Tuscany and Cambodia
- stood atop a Roman rooftop while thousands of birds flocked toward the Vatican overhead
- boated naked and dined (clothed) on the top of the Amalfi coast mountains
- hiked three hours to watch a sunset in Oia and woken the next day to cry tears of gratitude as I walked the streets of Greece at sunrise
- slept at six thousand feet among chickens on the floor of a makeshift barn

- hosted wine-fueled dinner parties in the Baja wine valley of Valle de Guadalupe
- gotten to know Mexican citizens, communities, and culture in ways the US rarely sees it (or portrays it)
- scaled limestone cliffs overlooking Thailand beaches
- spent countless hours on sleeper trains tied to all my luggage as the loveable "Lady Boys" gracefully propositioned anyone still awake
- spent an entire day driving a motorbike through the villages of rural Cambodia
- been the only female (so they say) ever to climb and jump off a seventy-foot pole into the Nam Song River
- cried tears of gratitude in the forests of the Swedish archipelago
- dodged men with Viking lineage as they smashed porcelain plates on adjacent walls in Paris (age twelve)
- pool-sharked men in their fifties (age ten)

And so much more.

I can tell you, my soul has been restored by seeing the world, and if this is something you've always dreamed of for yourself, please consider dropping this fuck right this very second.

Just go.

* * *

Entrepreneurship is hard for anyone. It is exponentially harder if you are female.

Years ago, when I started my second company, W3RKWELL,

people said all kinds of inappropriate things to me. I eventually developed a long list to keep a record of these statements. It wasn't to call anyone out; it was because I felt I needed to document it all and ask around to see if this was a normal occurrence for female business owners.

Some of the statements are included below:

"Wow, I love this kid's confidence." (I was standing directly next to him.)

"It probably isn't a good idea to start a company when you look like you're in your early twenties."

"If you can fix your taillight by yourself, it will show me that you're independent."

"I hope I'm not upsetting you with all these questions."

"My facts don't care about your feelings."

I posted the list on my personal Instagram account in an eyeroll moment. And then came the comments. The women were shocked but not shocked, and the men were confused.

"Some of these don't seem that inflammatory," said a male friend.

I agreed. It wasn't that people were rudely accosting me after my talks or degrading me or my work. It's that these things would never have been said to a man running a company.

Can you imagine a thirty-five-year-old man being told, in a

business development meeting, that if he could fix his own taillight he would be worthy of the contract? When I responded that I would imagine navigating years of world travel and purchasing a Southern California home at thirty-two years old (all by myself!) would be proof enough of my independence, he backpedaled in an effort to relieve his own ridiculousness and make me feel like I took it the wrong way (Fuck #3).

After I'd spent year or so working eighteen-hour days to build the W3RKWELL brand, two male colleagues from the behavior analytic community started hovering. Over the course of another year, they groomed me to believe I needed them, first praising me for my accomplishments and then diminishing them by showing me all the ways it could be better. Of course, they said they could help me continue to "the next level" and offered to invest in the company. They would need my business plan, access to all assets, and additional insight into where I would take the company over the next five years, all of which I gave them. We negotiated terms over several meetings, each time the same.

The day came to dot the i's and cross the t's on our formal contract. When we reviewed the terms once more, they were vastly different. *Eighteen percent* of the company would go to one investor's girlfriend for the role of "manager." This was not only a role we didn't need at the time, but it had also never been discussed, and it was as much as my three business partners had in total. The investor said he wanted a position for his girlfriend because, as he put it, "she's approaching forty and trying to start a yoga business, which, let's be honest, she'll be too old for soon."

I was livid and felt betrayed. I had already left my full-time job to focus on the influx of capital and grow relationships with potential clients. I immediately and angrily refused the offer, got off the phone, and cried for hours.

After this particular breakdown, I looked back on the previous year. It became increasingly clear that I had been groomed to believe I needed them if I wanted to be successful—that I couldn't and didn't know how to do it myself. The other investor managed to earn a "sales" role at the company for a few months. Not only did he fail to book a single client (I later realized that was never his intention), but he had no discernible skills or talent beyond making people *think* he did. When I became vocal about my concerns and pulled the deal, the investor who'd wanted his girlfriend included requested that I sign a nondisparagement and nondisclosure agreement. This was a request to silence me (Fuck #1). Our industry is extremely small, and we were running a book project, magazine, and side company with a dozen other behavior analysts who thought they were being "helped" by these individuals. I left it all and signed nothing.

While their manipulation was horrid, I failed to give weight to a few facts that would have likely kept me from this experience in the first place:

- My work was being broadcast on podcasts in one hundred countries and theirs was not.
- I had built a nationally recognizable brand and they had not.
- I had pioneered an entirely new concept by combining two emerging fields and they had not.
- I received weekly requests from people who wanted to be a part of my company, with some offering to work for free, and they did not.

When we allow others to let us believe we should depend on them, when we fail to understand what we bring to the table in life and at work, we risk buying into the belief that we need others, that we should wait for someone else, or that we should do it their way instead of believing in ourselves. In our vision. In our dreams. In business, travel, relationships, and the rest of what life has to offer.

I explore beyond the boundaries of my pre-approved life.

Fuck Being Dependent

Consider with curiosity:

- Have you ever wished you could see the world?
- Where would you go if you could go anywhere? What would you see or learn?
- Have you ever let anyone convince you that you couldn't do something yourself, like start a company or plan a dream trip? Why?
- When and with whom is being dependent rewarded?
- When and with whom is being independent rewarded?
- Where did your story of being dependent come from?
- What is maintaining it, and what are you getting from it?
- What is likely to happen if you keep this fuck?

YOUR REWRITE

In the following exercise, fill in the blanks when you feel inspired and clear. You can choose to commit to these new beliefs any time you're ready.

1. I'm dropping the belief that

....

....

2. Because

....

....

3. If I'm successful, (what will happen?)

....

....

4. If I'm successful, I will have time and energy for

....

....

5. And it will feel

....

....

6. My new belief is

....

....

7. And I will show this by (be specific: actions, words, phrases, etc.)

....

....

fuck #9

Be Fixed

"David, nobody cares."

—ALEXIS ROSE

Along with many growth-minded people I know, I have a few things I'm working on improving at any given time. I'm a personal growth warrior and happily take the stance that every single person on the planet is a work in progress, especially me.

However.

Have you ever carefully looked at the front of a magazine targeted to women? Regardless of the publication, the message is the same:

You are something to be fixed.

Whether it's an article on how to have a more peaceful home, how to get in shape, how to be a better partner, or how to cook the world's best something or other (I skip that part), they are all saying, "If you do this/buy this/become this, you will be happier, more peaceful, more attractive, etc. The reason you don't have the body you want (impossible beauty standards), hair you want (genes), relationship you want (life is not a movie), or home you want (constantly changing trends made to make you feel perpetually out of style) is because you aren't good enough. But don't worry. You can buy this and be fixed."

Entire industries were built on the backs of women who were made to believe that they were the problem. These industries thrive on women who live in a world that makes them feel unsure of how to be right, beautiful, confident, or enough.

Unhappy in your marriage? *Take this vacation and do these five things to be a better wife.*

Unhappy in your sex life? *Buy this product and wear this torture device to build your confidence.*

Feeling unattractive? *Buy this cream and restrict those calories.*

Feeling unsuccessful or inadequate? *Buy this bag, and post this picture, using this filter.*

I have several issues with these messages:

1. They drive commercialism in a way that takes advantage of women in need of something much more real, sustainable, and authentic.
2. They function as a temporary redirect and promise things they cannot possibly deliver.
3. They create additional stress by showing women what they

don't have but should have because other women have it (just look at this picture!).

At a recent dinner, I brought this "easy fix" concept up to a friend. He said, "That doesn't make sense. What does commercialism have to do with people's unhappiness? Money and supermodel girlfriends don't make people happy." I agreed. I don't know anyone who is happy *because* they have those things. But while thousands of books and articles exist to tell us that money and fame do not make us happy, we still *buy* as if they do. We still *behave* as though being happy simply requires a purchase of some sort, even though we intellectually know that is not the case.

Why?

Other people's fucks. And dopamine. But mostly other people's fucks. In my opinion, fucks perpetuated by the industries that need to sell stuff no one actually needs. Ask any marketing person what they sell, and most will tell you that while the products are always different, they are selling feelings or a way of life, not products. It flies in the face of commercialism to sell anyone on years of hard work, internal acceptance, and hard-won self-awareness in order to live the lives they truly desire.

Imagine the magazine ads:

Unhappy in your marriage? Spend months or years doing some hard work on yourself and with your partner to evaluate your goals, values, identities, needs, and communication patterns.

Unhappy in your sex life? Spend months or years doing hard work on yourself and with your partner to evaluate your goals, values, identities, needs, communication patterns, and weird but exciting fantasies.

Feeling unattractive? Evaluate years of your own learning history to better understand where your self-worth comes from and whether you still agree with valuing yourself based on your physical appearance. If you do, start getting better sleep, drinking more water, sticking to clean foods, and moving your ass every single day. If you don't, start all over and redefine your self-worth.

Feeling inadequate or unsuccessful? Evaluate years of your own learning history to better understand where your self-worth comes from and whether you still agree with valuing yourself based on your financial or intellectual success. If you do, start creating a new life for yourself by making very hard decisions on how to invest your time and energy.

SOAPBOX ALERT

How many times must we read about the "best way" to be healthy? Stop eating like an asshole, sleep, hydrate, move your body, and drop the fucks that send you into a weekly stress spiral. Done. If magazine editors truly wanted to be helpful, they would do well to help women evaluate what *leads* them to junk food and sedentary lifestyles in a root-cause analysis. They would be selling us babysitters, marriage counselors, life assistants, a healthy self-image, or a good hard look in the mirror that has nothing to do with new fucking shoes.

I was shocked when I heard a designer admit that there are now fifty-two "micro-seasons" of clothing per year. Stores like TopShop introduce four hundred new styles per week on their websites. These strategies are designed to make the consumer feel perpetually out of fashion after one week, thus parlaying that "never enough" feeling most of us carry around into big-time dollars for fast fashion companies.

I love fashion as much as the next woman, and there is some kind of magic that happens when I put on an outfit I feel confident in. That being said, researching this topic made me pause and take a more thoughtful perspective. I took some time to evaluate how and under what conditions I buy apparel and other items and how long the excitement stays with me after I've donned the perfect outfit to convey my mood and activities for the day.

I noticed this magic lasts approximately five to thirty minutes. The really pretty stuff gives me another boost the second time I wear it.

Despite the fact that I constantly tell myself not to buy more clothes, I always go back for more—usually much earlier than anticipated.

When? When I am feeling less than confident or capable or when I am bored with myself.

Do I enjoy it? No. It eventually brings on stress because I realize I didn't need whatever I purchased.

Then why do I do it? Because I am seeking ways to feel unique or I am under stress. Maybe my willpower reserve is low or making a purchase seems like a quick way to make myself feel special, confident, or noticeable to someone else.

I'm supposed to be above this. *Damn it.*

Interested to learn more about this phenomenon (and prove that I'm not the only irrational shopper out there), I did some research in the neuroscience literature. What I found was absolutely fascinating and changed not only the way I shop, but also the manner in which I purchase *any* item and even how I decide what to eat.

Robert Sapolsky, a neuroendocrinologist and professor of neurological sciences at Stanford, conducted an experiment with monkeys in order to study dopamine (the feel-good neurochemical) levels. He taught the monkeys that a reward was available by pairing it with a signal (think Pavlov's dogs). He then provided the reward when the monkey completed a task, and he continued the experiment to assess the effectiveness of reward schedules (rewards can be provided in a number of ways, called schedules, and they are critical for understanding behavior—for more information, please refer to the appendix).

Sapolsky hypothesized that a dopamine spike would occur when the reward was given (much like we get a dopamine spike when we find the perfect outfit or when someone likes our IG posts). The results were shocking. There was indeed a spike in dopamine when the reward was presented, but it paled in comparison to the excitement the monkeys experienced when they were simply notified a reward was *available*. He found that the monkeys experienced a dopamine spike when the *signal* for a reward was presented. In effect, receiving a reward did not cause nearly as much excitement as the *anticipation* of one.

Eager to try this in my own life, I paid attention while I planned my next dessert—something I indulged in rarely before my *Fuckless*ness kicked in. I was excited. I began reading through dessert menus at neighborhood restaurants, and I even became motivated to plan a longer run that day. When dessert finally came, I happily ate it. But even though this experiment required me to be more present with my food, I still didn't savor it. After the first two or three delicious bites, I snarfed it down and forgot I was eating it. My mind was elsewhere (probably searching for its next dopamine spike, honestly). It wasn't until a few hours later that I realized I'd had dessert for the first time in months and that I was no longer thinking about it. It didn't truly make me happier.

We buy things that excite us and make us feel like we are different than we are—better than we are—even if it's just for a few moments. They're little shots of excitement and possibility in a world where we crave attention and a feeling of belonging, but they provide none of these things in any real way. They make us feel temporarily whole, fixed, excited, acceptable.

After my research for this chapter, I began to purchase goods and clothes differently. I let go of what I felt I had to look like and what my home had to look like, and I accepted myself as a little less polished or formal if I wanted to be. No one noticed—or if they did, no one cared.

One day I showed up at a business meeting in a flannel, jeans, and a floppy hat. It was truly a *Fuckless* move, and it made me happy because I felt rebellious and it was what came to mind when I asked myself, *What do I really want to wear today?* The founder of the company complimented me and told me she was jealous of my cute and comfortable outfit.

Do you think you could wear only thirty-three items (i.e., shoes, jewelry, clothes) for three months? I wish I had birthed that idea myself, because it's pure genius.

Project 333 is about regaining the joy we miss out on when we agonize over what to wear. I caught wind of this concept through a documentary on minimalism. Among the comments from women who have tried it, the general consensus was that no one noticed.

A scene in *Schitt's Creek*, one of my all-time favorite shows for so many reasons, exemplified this perfectly. David was getting his driver's license, and his anxiety was through the roof (oh, that David). Among his projections about what would go wrong, what the driving instructor would think of him, and how he would eventually fail miserably, his sister, Alexis, set him straight:

"You are acting all sorts of crazy right now. This honestly *does not matter*. Nobody cares," Alexis said.

"Uh, people care," David argued. "I care. The driving examiner person cares."

Alexis responded, "No, he doesn't. Trust me. People aren't thinking about you the way that *you're* thinking about you."

It seems harsh, but I thought it was very accurate and freeing. It amused me to catch myself realizing that the repetitive worries in my mind—*What will they think if I wear this? How will I come off if I do this? What if my company doesn't make it?*—are wildly overestimated. I love freeing myself from this mental entrapment by reminding myself, *Nobody cares, Gia. Go do good work and enjoy your life.*

The insinuation that women are the problem and that we must fix ourselves to fit unrealistic or inaccurate standards does not stop or start with the fashion industry.

A few years ago, I put my hat in the ring to plan a series of leadership events for a friend's company. They said that they wanted to see more "high-potential" women in leadership roles, so I created a proposal for how they might do so.

I spoke with my friend before submitting my ideas:

"What constitutes *high potential*?" I asked.

"We don't know."

"You might want to flesh that out first. So what positions are available to women now?" I asked next.

"We don't have any openings."

"That would be another good place to start. What skills might these positions require?" I asked her next.

"We aren't sure."

She then sent me a picture of their last several training teams. All young white males.

I asked, "Does your company truly value diversity at all?"

"I don't know," my friend admitted. "They started this committee to plan female leadership events, but we aren't getting anywhere."

It was run by all women and overseen by the male CEO. They were given no additional time or compensation to get this committee and its events up and running, but they were given a decent budget (this immediately read as potential gender-washing for me). I didn't get the contract, but she shared the proposal from the company that did. The company was mostly women, and their proposal was a canned, three-part series including sessions entitled "Know Your Value," "Show Your Value," and "Grow Your Value."

"Well, this is enraging," I said to my friend.

"What do you mean?"

"Do you intend on getting fifty talented, high-potential women in a room to tell them that the reason they're not in leadership positions is because *they're* the problem?"

"Oh," she said. "Shit."

I also noted there were no men in the room. If women are to gain more opportunities for leadership positions and be successful across a variety of industries, this is an endeavor that involves *all* genders. We need to stop spending money on bullshit trainings and initiatives that teach women how to be completely different in order to be acceptable or worthy of a promotion.

A 2019 *HuffPost* article titled, "Women At Ernst & Young Instructed On How To Dress, Act Nicely Around Men," recounts a troubling scenario that occurred after the company faced its own public sexual harassment case. The message? Fix the women.

> Before the workshop, women were also given a "Masculine/ Feminine Score Sheet," which had them rate their adherence to stereotypical masculine and feminine characteristics both on the job and outside the office.
>
> The so-called masculine traits included "Acts as a Leader," "Aggressive," "Ambitious," "Analytical," "Has Leadership Abilities," "Strong Personality" and "Willing to Take a Stand."
>
> The so-called feminine traits included "Affectionate," "Cheerful," "Childlike," "Compassionate," "Gullible," "Loves Children" and "Yielding." None of the feminine traits involved leadership—ostensibly a focus of the training.

According to an attendee, the message was that women would be penalized if they failed to demonstrate female traits or if they behaved in a way more akin to the male traits. This is actually consistent with the double-bind in research, but it was the first I had heard of a training that encouraged women to stay in their place and step aside, so to speak.

Once again, the Glass Box. Act like a woman. But also, act like a man. But not too much like a man. And not too much like a woman either.

Smash the patriarchy, sure. There are archaic, systemic influences that certainly need to change. But this can also exacerbate the issue by positioning certain genders *against* each other. It also insinuates the patriarchy is linear and solely driven by men. This assumption does not help a society that has passed this fuck along to female leaders. These women had to compromise themselves and claw their way to the top of the patriarchal ladder, and since they've done so, they likely tote the same fuck men do: women need to fix themselves, to act like men.

A close friend of mine—let's call her Daviney—had a job that she was good at and that she loved. Her female boss continuously claimed she was a feminist but would also "help" her female team members by constantly telling them to "be T's (thinkers) instead of F's (feelers)." This comes from the Myers-Briggs assessment, which aggregates people into compartmentalized, tidy, wildly useless buckets.

She frequently commented on Daviney's clothes and asked when she was having children, to the point of awkwardness. Daviney said, "It got weird. It was like that was all she saw when she looked at me." Her boss would excuse low performance from males but demand twice as much from females. She even went so far as to deny a female employee's request to attend an event—a plea the employee made with a thoughtful plan about what she would learn and how it would add value to the team—and instead invite the employee's male counterpart, even though he did not ask to attend or put together any sort of plan.

Essentially, Daviney's boss was giving the women on her team the same messages regurgitated by society for decades. *You're the problem. Fix yourself. Be like a man.* This is why smashing the patriarchy (as much as I love smashing things) is not enough to completely derail the fuck that our global model of professional and capable is a white man who wears a suit. Telling people to "be a T instead of an F" goes against everything that person naturally is. It's another fuck given to some poor souls who now categorize "F" as wrong and "T" as right. Most people I know can manage to think *and* feel.

I hope to one day live in a world where a person showing up as their most authentic, wonderful self is valued. I suppose it starts with you deciding to do so right now. To me, that is how the world changes.

SOAPBOX ALERT

Women are typically treated as though they must act like men (but look very much like women) in order to be taken seriously, to be successful, or to stand a chance of being heard. But how does more of the same thinking and behaving benefit anyone? If innovation, creativity, compassion, and collaboration skills are of the highest value in the future of work, wouldn't it be true that we would benefit from articles and workshops on teaching men to act more like women?

Women have a wide variety of skillsets that require *zero* additional training, products, or services, and they should be leveraged, honored, and encouraged instead of suppressed or smashed down as unimportant. I know many women who try their hardest to "act like men" or "fix" what comes naturally to them because they've been made to feel that who they are is something that needs changing. They overfocus on their clothes, the way they walk, their emotions, their tone, their stance, the manner in which they share their ideas, *and* their actual performance. It's exhausting. When the result of this giant effort is being called aggressive, shrill, emotional, or controlling, it's punishment. It's oppressive. It hurts and it doesn't make sense. This is where women become angry and frustrated and more exhausted, all the while being expected to produce as much as individuals without this energy-sucking fuck.

I know you have likely been through this, and it just plain stinks. You tried to follow the rules and be agreeable, nice, and soft, and it didn't work. Then you tried the other way, and that didn't work either. This is your very own Glass Box. If your eyes are welling up right now, this might be a good fuck to drop. You will likely need to collect several other individuals to add power to this effort.

Please know that I'm *all for* purchasing things that are truly worth the investment. My point here is to sidestep the marketing wizards and do a little work to figure out what you actually enjoy and benefit from, outside the mindset of needing to be fixed.

If you feel perpetually behind in fashion, you're making purchases based on a feeling of "not good enough," or you purchase or receive trainings or other resources that teach you to be something else, this fuck needs to go.

*Their rules
are not a reflection
of my rightness.*

Fuck
Being Fixed

If this feels heavy at first, begin with the warm-up questions below:

- What is your favorite product, place, outfit, or service that truly makes you feel happy, beautiful, free, or fulfilled for more than a few minutes?
- What is your definition of self-care? Are products necessary?
- What is the number-one thing you have purchased for yourself in the past year that improved your confidence, health, or skills?

Then, consider with curiosity:

- When and with whom do you feel you have to fix yourself, or that you are not enough?
- When and with whom is being confident rewarded?

- Where did your story of being fixed or buying "a better you" come from?
- What is maintaining it, and what are you getting from it?
- What is likely to happen if you keep this fuck?

YOUR REWRITE

In the following exercise, fill in the blanks when you feel inspired and clear. You can choose to commit to these new beliefs any time you're ready.

1. I'm dropping the belief that

....

....

2. Because

....

....

3. If I'm successful, (what will happen?)

....

....

4. If I'm successful, I will have time and energy for

....

....

5. And it will feel

....

....

6. My new belief is

....

....

7. And I will show this by (be specific: actions, words, phrases, etc.)

....

....

Be Sexy...
but Sweet

"Boys will be, boys will be

Boys will be, boys will be boys

But girls will be women."

—DUA LIPA, "BOYS WILL BE BOYS"

We are wrapping up with a few fucks rolled into one overarching narrative:

Women are sexual beings first, wives and mothers second, and whatever else they choose to be after that third.

These roles operate in a frustrating, lose-lose, incompatible tension. This may be the biggest Glass Box we live in. While driving home from an LA restaurant where I was working on this piece, I had to pull over. My body was tense and irritable, and I wanted to scream. I didn't even know why. I came to a halt after nearly hitting the curb, got out, and squatted on the sidewalk, holding myself while I cried. It brought up a lot of emotion and pain for me, so please take this last chapter slowly and with support.

I chose politics for the first of these examples because the gendered storyline is extremely strong here. It also highlights a huge gap in who has decision-making power when it comes to abortion, taxes, mandated parental leave, and many other decisions that affect our day-to-day lives. A shocking percentage of our country is still grappling with the fact that women should have decision-making power over their own bodies (looking at you, Texas), much less have every right to hold offices that give them power (Fuck #3), and the oppression for women in these roles is extremely concerning. Over the past few years, I've noticed that where men are attacked for their political history and lack of experience or policies, women are frequently attacked for traits pertaining to them being women.

I remember when it was uncovered that President Bill Clinton had a sexual relationship with Monica Lewinsky. I heard many adults around me say things like, "He doesn't have to be a good husband; he's a good president."

So if Vice President Kamala Harris received oral sex from an intern, we'd all be saying the same thing, right?

In 2019, Republican politician Robert Foster, who was running for Mississippi governor, refused to let a female reporter ride with him in his car without a male chaperone.

In an interview he explained his reasoning:

Perception is reality in this world. And I did not want there to be a perception that I was riding with another female and that something was—promiscuous going on or anything like that.

That's fair, he wanted to protect himself, you might be thinking.

The reporter's response:

Let's talk about the perception of impropriety—this idea that if a woman is photographed with a man, it could be perceived as, you know, an inappropriate relationship. Well, that only happens if you see this reporter who's doing her job as a sexual object first and a reporter second.

Like most gendered narratives, we have to ask ourselves, "Would this same assumption be true for a female candidate and a male reporter?" What if RBG or AOC refused to ride in cars alone with men, stating that the assumption would be that they were sleeping together or that the male reporter would sexually assault her? Can you imagine the backlash?

"Don't flatter yourself, honey."

"She's not fit for the job."

"She's not professional enough."

"She's crazy."

The sexual lens through which we first view women is undeniable. From celebrities to everyday individuals, we make statements about a woman's behavior (perceived, real, or imaginary) and appearance as if she asked for our opinion or as if it relates to her professional competence, when we don't do anywhere near the same to men.

Alexandria Ocasio-Cortez has been criticized for appearing in *Vanity Fair* wearing a $1,000 suit, dancing, and her stunning sense of fashion. Let's call this what it is: a gorgeous young woman of color rising up and shining through. And to lesser, easily threatened folks who believe women like her should tone it down and stay out of the men's jobs, it's a slap in the face.

If you are a confident, capable woman who doesn't happen to look like AOC or care about fashion, buckle up.

When asked about Angela Merkel's choice of attire during a meeting with Barack Obama, designer Karl Lagerfeld stated, "Miss Merkel [should dress] according to her special proportions. The proportions were bad, like the cut. The pants were too long." Merkel has received other offhand criticisms for her attire, like when she wore the same dress to an annual music event in 2012 as she wore four years prior.

The horror.

The veteran German chancellor responded in summation, "It's no problem at all for a man to wear a dark blue suit for a hundred days in a row, but if I wear the same blazer four times in two weeks, that leads to letter writing from citizens."

Letter writing! About fashion concerns.

Can you imagine giving such attention to the late Steve Jobs or Facebook's Mark Zuckerberg for wearing the exact same thing *every day*?

Thrive Global did. In a recent article, Vincent Carlos wrote:

> Simply put, every decision you make uses up your mental energy. Just the simple act of thinking about whether you should choose A or B will tire you out and reduce your brainpower. This means that the more decisions you have to make throughout the day, the weaker your decision making process will become.
>
> This is why many successful individuals like Steve Jobs, Mark Zuckerberg and Albert Einstein decided to reduce the amount of decisions they make throughout the day by doing things such as choosing to adopt a monotonous wardrobe.
>
> They understood that less time spent on making decisions meant more brain power and time for everything else.

I read this article and genuinely questioned whether or not I'd had a stroke.

When I did a search using the phrase "Angela Merkel wears same outfit to save brainpower" the first page included articles titled, "Angela Merkel Has Been Wearing the Same Tunic for 18 Years," "GASP! Germany's Merkel Is An Outfit Repeater," and "Angela Merkel Wears Same Holiday Outfit 5 Years Running."

Only one link by style and image coach Gail Morgan mentioned anything about saving time, and it was still depressingly gendered:

Some women have adopted this simple wardrobe approach—for example Angela Merkel—buttoned up jackets and simple necklaces; or Hilary Clinton—mainly trouser suits—but both of these women still wear a variety of colours which will hinder their ability to make quick choices. Many women when limiting their colour choices will just focus on black, which is not always the best solution because head to toe black can create a barrier and be very alienating (Victoria Beckham uses this technique very successfully!) it is also quite a hard colour and therefore isn't flattering to all complexions.

This tells women, "Sure, you can try relieving yourself of this time-sucking burden you don't enjoy, but it still won't be as flattering or acceptable as if you wasted all your brainpower on colorful outfits, because that is your worth."

Again, imagine the men mentioned in this section being ousted for wearing the same outfit:

"Well, Barack Obama gave the State of the Union address wearing the same blue suit as he wore two years ago. I dunno, Bill. I'm genuinely concerned for our country."

"Bill Gates took the stage at a TED event this week, shocking the crowd by wearing a *pink sweater.*"

I'd imagine the response would be something like, "Who cares? Can he run the country or his company?"

The same *HuffPost* article about the disastrous Ernst & Young training I mentioned in the previous chapter reviewed the "self-improvement" advice for female attendees:

One section of the document is devoted to women's appearance: Be "polished," have a "good haircut, manicured nails, well-cut attire that complements your body type," it states on Page 36. But then, a warning: "Don't flaunt your body—sexuality scrambles the mind (for men and women)."

The most important thing women can do is "signal fitness and wellness," the presentation continues.

Jane recalls being told that if you want men to focus on the substance of what you're talking about, "don't show skin." If you do, men are less likely to focus "because of sex," Jane recalls being told. The advice made her "feel like a piece of meat," she said.

The ridiculousness continued:

Attendees were even told that women's brains are 6% to 11% smaller than men's, Jane said. . . . Women's brains absorb information like pancakes soak up syrup so it's hard for them to focus, the attendees were told. Men's brains are more like waffles. They're better able to focus because the information collects in each little waffle square.

I assume the women were instead focusing their brainpower on colorful, flattering outfits that signaled fitness but not sexuality so as to avoid eliciting a sea of boners everywhere they went.

Once again, a woman is given the additional mental responsibility of considering everyone else before she acts, while I assume nearly zero men stand in front of their closets thinking, *What will they think of me if I wear this tie? Will they take me seriously? Or will they see me as fresh meat and ask me to a "business dinner"?*

I have many gorgeous, fit girlfriends who jump on their Pelotons and—among home projects, partners, kids, and work—kick their own ass every day and have toned bodies as a result. But when it's time for the pool party or to dress up for dinner and drinks, they hide themselves from the world because it's simply too uncomfortable to stand out now that they are wives and mothers. Whether it's because they have children and their identities are magically supposed to change, or because they attract uncomfortable stares (I have seen this myself), it's enough for them to change their lifestyles. And it's not only the men gawking; it is more often than not other women.

Please read this next part carefully.

If you are triggered by another woman's sexuality—if you see a gorgeous, confident woman and automatically dislike her or project negative intent upon her, whether it be a toned body, pretty face, or *Fuckless* ownership over her sexuality or effortless sense of fashion—this is a *you* issue.

I'll say it again.

This. Is. A. You. Issue.

We are taught to assume that women who show interest in looking good, who are confident, or who embrace sexuality are *intentionally* trying to make us feel insecure, possess a threatening and seductive agenda, or have malicious intent.

Unfortunately, a few of my girlfriends have been cheated on, as have I. One of the hardest things for me to hear during these times is how ugly, fat, etc. the other woman is. I know it feels good to shit on the person who was involved in hurting you, and cheating is always so painful. But the uncomfortable, unpopular thing I have to point out is that it's not the other woman's fault, no matter how much society and movies want you to believe it. She did not agree to be faithful to you; he did. She did not tie him up and force herself upon him—unless she did, and then by all means go slash some tires. This isn't a discussion on whether to take someone back or not. That's a choice you both have to make. This is simply a point to remind us where to focus attention when these unfortunate circumstances occur.

When females hold a primary role as sexual beings, there are harmful consequences. If the majority of people, from teenagers to full-blown adults, agree to this fuck (consciously or unconsciously), we also agree to the fuck that men can't help themselves and *aren't expected to.*

"She asked for it. Did you see how she was dressed?"

"She didn't say no, so it couldn't have been assault."

"She was acting fine afterward, so it couldn't have been that bad."

"What did you expect him to do? He's a guy."

Women aren't only given the responsibility of thinking about everyone else first; they are also given the responsibility for other people's actions, regardless of propriety, reality, or logic:

- for "asking for it," because she dresses in a way that society tells her she should
- for "not saying no" but looking and acting extremely hesitant

and uncomfortable in a society that tells her she's overre-
acting
- for "not speaking up" in a society that tells her to be quiet
- for not being believed once she does speak up in a society
  that tells her she is wrong and mistaken
- for fooling around with the boss in a society of aggressive,
  narcissist leaders who manipulate, lie, and take before she
  knows what hit her
- for being a confident, sexual being in a society that tells her
  to cover up because she's a mother now

While these fucks didn't come *from* you, you may hold them
in your belief system, even unknowingly, and you are certainly
affected by them.

On the similar topic of female confidence, in my own life I realized I'd been surrounded by older women—mostly the private
school mothers I grew up around—who made nasty comments
about other women who clearly intimidated them. I heard comments like "She thinks she's so wonderful," and "Who does she
think she is?" which signaled that the woman in question's
behavior was wrong and intentionally meant to piss off and
diminish everyone around her. My young self thought, *I don't
understand. What is she doing?* It felt wrong, but I took it on
because those around me taught me that female confidence was
an affront to women everywhere and something to be avoided.

Once I realized that judging confident or overtly beautiful
women was making *me* look bad, this one was easy to let go
of. I knew exactly where it came from and that it wasn't mine,
and it made me feel gross because it was so misaligned with my
values. It also defied logic. I reframed my internal language and

taught myself to immediately tease out what was so triggering about whoever I encountered, and then I tried to emulate that quality myself. For example, if old voices said, *Who the hell does she think she is?* I would ask myself, *What is she doing that is making me feel this way?* If the answer was, *She projects a confidence in her walk and posture*, then I would practice walking like I ruled the world.

This is what happens when you become a behavior analyst. Everything and everyone becomes a giant, exciting puzzle piece.

Not only did I get to drop this belief fast, but there was an interesting side effect. I created a real-world, behavior-based training on skills and actions that I wanted and admired. I actually created new habits born from my original ugly feelings.

There were also some less-desirable side effects. I began to intimidate and threaten others in the same way I was initially intimidated and threatened. Unfortunately, not everyone in my life was ready to see this fuck for what it truly was: their stuff.

Over dinner with a friend, I received some well-intended advice:

"You need to understand how you come off to people. You are very confident, and you have to understand how that makes others feel."

She went on to insinuate I should manage and tone down my confidence so it would make other people feel more comfortable. I was triggered again, but this time I couldn't use my trick. I saw no behavior I wanted to emulate; I was offended and hurt and felt a sense of injustice. No one tells men to be less confident because of how it affects other people. We reward the shit out of them for self-aggrandizing and grandstanding at work, at home, and in life.

Instead, I responded, "I've done a lot of work to become this confident, and I'm not diminishing that because other people haven't."

We *learn* to be hesitant or confident, soft or strong, loud or quiet, which means that we can *unlearn* those things and replace them with something that better suits us. Getting angry with a woman for possessing a trait you do not is just plain lazy. Drop the fucks keeping you from being that thing and go *learn* it! There is no patent on sexuality, confidence, or anything else you want to be.

When we lash out at a woman who triggers us, most of the time we are simply angry that we play by "the rules" and she doesn't. She calls her own shots because she understands that this is her life. And that can create a mirror in which we see ourselves failing to do so. We feel bad, and we project that feeling onto her as if she woke up that morning on a mission to launch psychological warfare on our lives.

Calling another woman fat doesn't make you skinnier. Calling her dumb doesn't make you smarter. Asking, "Who does she think she is?" doesn't highlight her shortcomings; it highlights *yours*. Let's agree to let amazing women inspire us instead of intimidate us.

While I'm making calls to action, let's also stop calling women who go without makeup or who wear a bikini after age thirty "brave." She's not fucking brave. Why are those things brave?

Because she's going out into the world without preparing to accommodate meaningless expectations set by total strangers? No. She is simply deciding where she'd rather spend her time that day, and it's not going to be on appealing to the masses. She is unaffected, which gives her grace.

And while there's a worthy discussion full of OSMs when it comes to women's "visual value," the clothes a woman chooses aren't the biggest issue. It's that, when we primarily focus on how women visually present to the world, *we diminish and discount everything else about them.* This is how we come to see women as sexual beings first—as visual beings whose value comes in what the world first sees and finds acceptable—instead of for their desires, how they think and feel about things, and their ideas, skills, talents, and power.

This fuck is similar to pieces of Fuck #9 (Be Fixed) but goes the extra step into the unwinnable tug-of-war women face when they are first viewed as visual, sexual objects.

An article by Rhonda Garelick in *The Cut* stated this concept beautifully:

> As all professional women know, there is no sartorial or visual "neutral" for us—no fully unobtrusive uniform that will let us blend completely into the background. No matter what clothes we choose, we are "curating" ourselves, selecting from a seemingly infinite array of options—all of which will be scrutinized for meaning. Skirts or trousers, sexy or serious, long or short, boho or glam—whichever we settle on, we can never enjoy the anonymous simplicity and instant, uncomplicated authority of a man in a suit.

This is because women are the "visible" sex, the half of the species whose visual surface is constantly on display and fragmented into countless smaller sections to be adorned, revered, scrutinized, or reviled.

Read: there is no winning here. So tomorrow morning, challenge yourself. Stand in front of your closet and say, "Fuck it. What do I want to wear today?"

Then go do it.

I do this every day, and it's *lovely*. On days when I catch myself overthinking an outfit, I realize I am irritable, flustered, and hurried because it's not where I want to be spending my energy and I am in the thick of making an inauthentic choice. Oddly enough, when I go out into the world as myself, I get noticed more for doing so. Not in a sexual way, but in a "Huh, you really do what you want" kind of amusement and appreciation. I also like to believe it gives others permission to be comfortable and redefine how they visually show up to the world if they choose to care about doing so (remember, either way, no judgment. This is your belief to keep, drop or alter).

We've reviewed the role sexuality plays in women's experiences and expectations in their careers. Let's take a look at two other areas: *wife* and *mother*.

When I lived in DC, I had fancy, important friends that took me to parties and pushed me in front of fancy, important people in an effort to get me photography gigs. At one particular party I was introduced to a married couple who shared the following information:

- They had children.
- They loved their children.
- They took annual trips to get away from their children on "remember why we got married" vacations.
- These vacations included sex toys, sex chairs, and sexy costumes.

I will never stop loving the way East Coasters will unapologetically, bluntly put it out there like it ain't no thing. I was fascinated and, because of their openness, followed up with all kinds of personal and inappropriate questions.

When I asked them how their sexual identities changed from dating to marriage to being parents, they looked at each other and laughed.

"We've had to keep each other in it every week for the last fifteen years."

I asked what "in it" meant.

The wife responded, "We committed to treating each other as sexual beings, regardless of where we were in other life roles, as much as we could. We both value sex heavily and did not want to lose the part of our relationship that was just for us among jobs, kids, and the like."

After years of hearing the same refrains of "We don't have time for sex," or "I don't feel sexy anymore," I was amazed and impressed.

The man chimed in, "One time, she even flat out said, 'You're getting fucking boring, honey!' I went right to the [sex] toy store."

He wasn't embarrassed. He wasn't threatened. He was bought in. He appreciated the nudge because they had both decided sexual identity within the context of their lives was important and, therefore, they *should* hold each other accountable.

I broached the topic of sex vacations in my own (childless) relationships and marriage for the next seven years, with little success. I became confused as to why I was valued and chased for my looks and sexuality my entire life, but when I became the serious girlfriend or wife and *I* made the suggestions and wanted to be adventurous and weird, it was perceived as off-putting.

This is an example of the lose-lose Glass Box of sexuality women face, especially as wives and mothers.

Ludacris said it best: "We want a lady on the street, but a freak in the bed."

But maybe only when it's *their* idea.

Let's talk about one of my favorite behavioral phenomena, *counter control.*

Behavior is both a result of the environment and a source of control over it, and counter control is most often resistance or refusing to "give in" in an effort to regain control.

Essentially, it looks like this:

Person A says, "Honey, I really love it when you [sexually deviant behavior here]."

Person B becomes resistant to the request and, in an effort to retain control, does not fulfill the fun, sexually deviant request.

It sounds like Person B is just being a dick for no reason, but I can't tell you how many times I've had and watched my friends have versions of this same conversation.

I'm what you'd call a hopeless romantic (emphasis on hopeless), and in every single relationship I've had since high school, I've asked for exactly what I wanted (nicely) because I grew up with lots of male friends who constantly complained that women are confusing and don't ask for what they want. In return, my partners thanked and assured me that romantic gestures, sex adventures, or the like were all on their way.

After several weeks or months of excitedly waiting, nothing. I would bring it up again, nicely. Every time, it went like this:

"I don't want you to have to tell me what to do. I want to do it on my own."

Well, then why the fuck haven't you just—Okay, patience, Gianna.

I would say okay and smile patiently.

More weeks would go by.

"Hey, babe?" I would say. "Remember that conversation we had about…?"

"I *told you* I don't want you to nag me about it!" he would respond.

"Then why don't you just do it?"

And then one or both people would be pissed. I didn't get what I asked for nicely, so I asked again, less nicely, and my partner had their resistance highlighted, making the counter control stronger. It's an emotionally immature tug-of-war that sucks the soul out of the relationship. Now *no one* wants to get naked.

In one relationship in particular I was made to feel needy, and as a result, I felt crazy, so I took some data.

Each time I brought up a specific desire, we had a two- to three-hour discussion on why I wanted it, which culminated in my partner saying now they understood it and wanted it too. Two to three months would pass without the desire being fulfilled for either of us, and I would bring it up again, with the same response. This pattern continued for eighteen months.

At some point, counter control is so strong that one party gives up.

Is it you?

Is there something, or many things, in your relationship that you desire, but you're too afraid of bruising an ego, making someone feel bad, or sounding—how do I put this —slutty?

In 2012, when Georgetown law student Sandra Fluke argued that birth control should be covered by insurance, talk show host Rush Limbaugh lashed out, calling her a "slut" and a "prostitute" on air:

> What does it say about the college co-ed Susan Fluke [sic], who goes before a congressional committee and essentially says that she must be paid to have sex, what does that make her? It makes her a slut, right? It makes her a prostitute. She wants to be paid to have sex. She's having so much sex she can't afford the contraception. She wants you and me and the taxpayers to pay her to have sex. What does that make us? We're the pimps.

First, whether you have sex once a year or forty-five times a day, you take the exact same number of birth control pills per day—one. Second, there was seemingly no conscious thought about the fact that contraceptives protect men from having unwanted children too. Third, the quick ride from wanting to avoid having children to "being paid to have sex" demonstrates how threatening women's control over their own sexuality and body are to certain individuals. Fourth, Limbaugh seemed to be unaware that medical treatment for his excessive smoking and, as a result, lung cancer (which eventually killed him and may have affected the health of those around him, unlike sex), would also be covered by insurance, and no one was causing an uproar about that.

When women own their sexuality, ask for what they want, or talk about sex in the way that men do, it goes against the standard fuck that women are meant to wait for men to initiate (see also, Fuck #7, Be Chosen), to swallow their desires, and to appear whatever version of ladylike the world has for them at the moment. Married women are expected to tone it down in public, if not with their clothing, then with their personality.

Flirting harmlessly, being overtly sexual, or owning that "feeling herself" vibe sends awkward stares around the room.

When I went from engaged to married, I noticed a change in some friends. I received calls and invites from married women more often, and my single friends didn't reach out as much. I realized my life was supposed to change. *I* was supposed to change. I was in a different role simply because I'd chosen to sleep with one person instead of however many I wanted. As a natural flirt who was now a wife, this was hard for me. I was voted "Class Flirt," which always amused me. In a room of one hundred people, the one person I'm not talking to is the person I'm interested in. But because I was an extroverted, vivacious, cute girl, everyone assumed I wanted to bone whoever I happened to be speaking to at the moment, which was always everyone.

Using my peers in rural Pennsylvania as a barometer, I was sexually conservative. I was, according to the boys around me, a "tease." I was raised with serious warnings about what boys and men would want from me (my body) and therefore learned to constantly play defense. As I write this sentence, I am thirty-nine years old and have never made the first move or asked someone out on a date. Playing offense, like making the first move or saying I liked someone before they said it first, seemed very risky. I learned I had power, and I liked to wield it. But I wasn't about to give it away. I learned that once you did, the allure was gone. Your power was taken. You'd served your purpose.

Funny enough, I never received warnings about men stealing my intellectual property or using me for my ideas, which has become the bane of my existence as both an academic and businesswoman.

After earning several advanced degrees, starting a few companies, and building myself as a brand—twice, thanks to COVID-19—I heard zero warnings about people using me for my brain. I did, however, hear lots of surprise in people's voices when I told them about my work and what I did for a living.

"Wow, you have your own business? You started it yourself?"

It's not that this is a bad thing, per se, but it's certainly infantilizing, and always with the underlying tone of surprise that a woman could be relatively attractive and smart enough to start her own company. Imagine a thirty-nine-year-old man telling a group at a cocktail party that he has his own company, and hearing, "Wow! You started a company all by yourself?" in a tone typically reserved for a nine-year-old who just made the honor roll.

It goes against socio-normative expectations for women to be breadwinners or business owners. And if the woman happens to be attractive, it's almost against the rules. Add "married" or "mom" to that story and, yikes, Glass Box judgment all around. No matter where she spends her time—at work, as a mother, or as a wife—someone has something to say about it. It's never enough, and if she has a male partner, he most likely has very different expectations (and is more likely to be chastised for wanting to spend time with his family over drinks with the boss).

That woman has to deal with significantly more bullshit than a man in her position because she dared to defy the continuously perpetuated order:

1. sexual being
2. wife/mother
3. whatever she has time for afterward

Essentially, it seems as though women are fucked, no matter what.

You might be feeling completely deflated by now. This is heavy stuff, so feel it if that's what comes up for you. But there is hope! In my experience, times of high emotion are also times that signal a change may be necessary, so it's time to see if this is a fuck you'd like to drop. Taking control over your own narratives, actions, and beliefs here will no doubt help you rise up and feel empowered instead of deflated. I'd argue this is one of the most difficult fucks to explore and drop because it's so ingrained in our society, other women, and even ourselves. But that doesn't mean it can't be done. This can change, and it starts with you.

I want to round out this chapter by saying that it was the hardest for me to write. I realized how much time and effort I'd spent focused on fulfilling my primary role as something to be watched and looked at instead of listened to or intellectually interested in. I felt overwhelming sadness at how much time I felt I'd lost being focused on something that didn't truly matter to me.

This became shockingly evident as I was writing the last few pages of this chapter while sitting in an LA coffee shop. A man sitting across from me struck up a conversation as I was deep in writing mode (annoying). We continued to talk, and I shared that I was a behavior scientist. He continued to share that he was in the social sciences as well, and it opened up a conversation about this chapter. He even sent me research from his female colleagues on gender-based power imbalances in business.

As I was getting up to leave, he asked me to the Hollywood Bowl to see a concert. Up to this point, there was only intellectual conversation—most of which was focused on how women are valued based on their sexual appeal instead of their ideas and career success—and he heralded me for my work and writing such a "necessary" book. I took a few days to think about it but eventually accepted the invitation. Almost immediately, I started receiving texts from him.

When I mentioned that I was writing about women struggling with their sexuality, he responded, "Well, it looks like you've got that part down."

When I told him I'd be wearing jeans and a T-shirt to the concert, he texted back, "With a figure like that, you can wear what you want."

Really.

I'm used to these comments from men, but it felt invasive and awful coming from a person with whom I had been vulnerable and shared my thoughts about female sexuality and the challenges we face.

This is where some people might say, "He was just complimenting you."

Let's put this into perspective according to value and gendered roles.

Imagine meeting a very rich person, and let's say that person is a man. Society tells him he's a great catch because he is financially successful. You find this success attractive, so you compliment his wealth by saying "I hear you're very successful" with a flirty smile. He might love it, and that's great. He's probably worked really hard. But let's say you go out on a date, and you continue to compliment his bank account and overfocus on his wealth by saying things like "Your Rolex is amazing," "I *love* your Benz," and "It's such a turn-on that you can afford this place." At some point, the man is going to question if you *only* value his wealth. He might feel bad because he wants to be seen for more than his money, which is understandable.

We call this being a gold-digger, and it's a bad thing.

So what do we say about a man who places a primary value and focus on women's sexuality?

We say, "He's just being a guy."

As you may have guessed, it's not just a few bad male apples toting this fuck. When I moved to San Diego for a promotion, I was tasked with shadowing a supervisor while learning the ropes. Although she was supposed to be training me, within three weeks I was given the uncomfortable role of supervising her. Not only that, but I was also told I would now be managing all of the supervisors in my region. For a man, this would have been awesome. In my case, I winced.

I had spent dozens of extra hours unfucking treatment binders, reviewing data, and correcting behavior plans according to updated science. I went above and beyond because I loved my job, and coming from the East Coast, "above and beyond" was just the expectation. It wasn't that I didn't deserve the promotion; it was the repercussions I knew were coming.

I asked my boss if we could give it more time and added that I thought such a fast move up the ranks would piss people off. Regardless of my call, I was moved into the position I had earned. However, within weeks, the women under me became obstinate and disrespectful toward me. When I brought this up to my boss, with whom I had a great relationship, she laughed and said, "It's because you're overtly attractive."

I stopped wearing makeup, traded my fancy Washington, DC, attire for flipflops and leggings, and tried to fly as far under the radar as possible. Absolutely nothing changed. I went back to my boss and told her my attempts failed and asked her what else I could do.

She sighed and said, "There's nothing you can do about it, Gianna."

I told this story for four years. One day, a friend of mine said, "It's interesting that she said your looks were the problem and not the fact that you're exceptional at your job."

My mind was blown. It had never occurred to me that even among other women, I was primarily viewed as something who is seen instead of someone who thinks. And I was fucked for both.

Right about now, as with every chapter I've written, is where this fuck gets into my head.

You might be thinking, *She's nailing this fuck!*

You also might be thinking, *She's just bitter.*

She sounds conceited.

She's why feminism gets a bad name.

If so, you might be carrying this fuck too. I have no problem being complimented or having my looks noticed. I *do* have a problem when a male stranger makes uninvited comments about my body, when most of the attention and compliments I receive are physical in nature, or when my skills and efforts are overshadowed by my outfits. I like looking good. I adore fashion, and I'm a very sexual person. I've also worked really hard to learn, build a few businesses, travel, and have an impact on the world. To me, the latter are exponentially more interesting than the former.

I know you feel the same way about your own talents, dreams, and experiences. I love to imagine a world where our first instinct is to tell little girls (and big girls) they look smart or adventurous instead of pretty.

It's not that sexuality doesn't matter, if you want it to, or that being sexy is an abhorrent thing. It's that when we treat women and girls as if it's *all* that matters or the first thing that matters, we reinforce things that, at the end of the day, are much less important than their contributions to the world. When we overvalue sexuality or make women feel like their work and non-family contributions to the world come last, we screw them (and society) out of the talent, gifts, and effort they bring to the table.

Additionally, we would benefit from rethinking the value we place on men's financial wealth and success. I've watched many men struggle to be "enough" based on their bank accounts or cut ethical corners—doing downright disgusting and morally corrupt things in the process—in order to obtain and then protect the level of success society tells them they should have. What if we started valuing men based on how kind, mindful, or helpful they are?

What gets rewarded gets repeated. And if we want to see more productive, positive actions, we have to treat them as *more* important than an individual's sexuality or wealth for their behavior to follow. It's a complete paradigm shift, but the benefits could be staggering. We would very likely see vast improvements in women's mental health, gender equality in the workforce, changes in entertainment and media, and more compassionate male leaders and partners, to name a few.

If you're sick of playing sexy for society, if you want to be sexy *and* have a family but feel tension, if your sexual desires are going largely unmet in your relationship, or if you have a burning desire to reframe your sexuality altogether, this is the perfect time to drop this fuck.

This chapter was *a lot*, but you made it. Here are a few warm-ups to guide your next exercise:

- Do you value being sexy? If so, how much effort are you willing to put in?

- When do you feel sexiest?
- How much time and effort do you spend in a sexually oriented role compared to time and effort spent being smart, strong, interesting, funny, or a good friend?
- When was the last time someone noticed your adventurous spirit, sensitive nature, or baller work ethic? Was it noticed or rewarded as strongly as other, possibly physical attributes of yours?
- When you are spending time with a romantic interest or partner, what do you compliment them for?
- When you spend time with young people and children, what behaviors or traits do you encourage?
- Consider your favorite non-physical quality. Do you receive attention for this quality more or less often than physical qualities?

*My worth extends far beyond the borders
of sexuality and a supporting role.*

Fuck Being Sexy...but Sweet

Consider with curiosity:

- When do you feel truly sexy? With whom is your version of sexy appreciated?
- When and with whom do you feel you must conform or become an inauthentic version of sexy?
- Where did your story of being sexy come from?
- What is maintaining it, and what are you getting from it?
- What is likely to happen if you keep this fuck?

YOUR REWRITE

In the following exercise, fill in the blanks when you feel inspired and clear. You can choose to commit to these new beliefs any time you're ready.

1. I'm dropping the belief that

....

....

2. Because

....

....

3. If I'm successful, (what will happen?)

....

....

4. If I'm successful, I will have time and energy for

....

....

5. And it will feel

....

....

6. My new belief is

....

....

7. And I will show this by (be specific: actions, words, phrases, etc.)

....

....

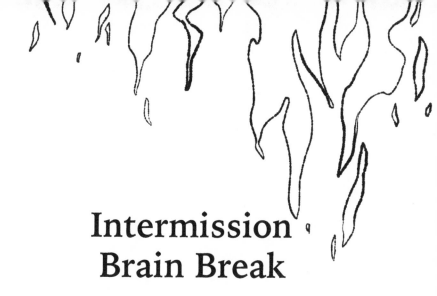

Intermission
Brain Break

Throughout my research, interviews, and putting my lived experience on replay, an enormously important question arose. Now that you're through the heaviest content in the book, you're ready for it.

If gender narratives and labels have functioned mostly to hold us back, hurt us, or create unnecessary and unfounded limits to our careers and lives, *what is the point of them?*

As you move into Part 2, consider this question if it resonates with you. You might find that it will help you to keep perspective and grounding as you take your *Fuckless*ness out into the world. You may encounter some confused, jealous, or frustrated individuals whose faces seem to say, *Women don't do it that way.*

If we can consider the statement above, we can begin to ask "Why not?"

Part Two

Living (and Staying) Fuck-Free

As the author of this book, I feel a deep responsibility to not only help you drop what's dragging you down to bring the best of you back to life, but to also help you keep it that way. It is my sincere wish that this book inspires you, but if it doesn't also help you to make positive, *sustainable* changes that lead to your fulfillment and happiness, then I've failed.

Let's talk about what it's going to be like when you take your *Fuckless*ness out into the world.

Show You
What You're
Made Of

I make a good amount of money standing on a stage doing what I do best: talking. After a few years, I realized that my role was to spew science while being entertaining, maybe even a little inspiring, but I was troubled by the question of whether my words and ideas had a lasting impact. I didn't want to be a dancing monkey on a stage; I wanted to be a dancing monkey that shook shit up and changed things for the better.

I decided to make two changes: I doubled my speaking fees and added four months of advisory-style "impact sessions" to increase the likelihood that whatever I said while on stage had continued impact. It made my work much more effective because while people originally walked away from my talks thinking, *That's a great idea. I'm so pumped*, they walked back into the same, unchanged environment on Monday.

And that just wasn't something I wanted to be a part of. With this change, I got to hang around and make sure things got better. If I'm putting my energy into something, it's going to cause a ripple.

And I *know* you didn't do all this work to return to the status quo.

You are now a ripple. When you change, it changes others, if only how they treat you in return. But the change only lasts if the ripple isn't afraid to make a tiny splash. The fact that you're still reading this means you already have everything you need. My legal team tells me it's creepy and ill-advised to follow you around to make sure your changes stick, so this is where I gently place responsibility upon your shoulders to carry on.

You're a goddamn warrior, and I believe in you.

Now that you've reviewed all the false beliefs holding you back, let's check in:

- How are you feeling?
- What has reviewing the list of fucks revealed to you about yourself?
- Was there one fuck that stood out—or many?
- Make some notes about whatever comes up for you here:

....

....

....

Regardless of the number of fucks holding you down, I know you've got at least one you're dedicating energy and space to dropping.

Smile like you know what's coming, because I'm smiling for you as I type this in a Santa Cruz coffee shop (seriously, I look deranged).

Today, you'll start making different decisions about how you live your life. Today, you'll continue to set an example for your children or your friends or your coworkers—but most importantly, yourself. Today, you'll start to change the world for females, and maybe all humans, in a seriously meaningful way. How cool is that?

Being *Fuckless* in the privacy of one's own home is easy(ish). It's the rest of the world that derails us, bless their hearts. It is not enough to be inspired and to have clarity on the change we want to make. We must actually live it, over and over, every single day. That means going out into the world rooted, clear, confident, and armed with the tools necessary to stand tall in a world that tries to keep you seated.

When we are not given the skills to protect who we've become, we are in danger of drifting back to who we were.

In this section I will give you *five ways* to carry all this hard work with you for years to come. They are:

1. identifying values
2. redistributing energy
3. weighing alternatives

4. using language signals
5. regifting

But first, let's talk about *vulnerability*—a critical component in the depth and success of this process.

According to Brené Brown, being vulnerable requires "uncertainty, risk, and emotional exposure." As a behavior analyst, and knowing that behavior is bidirectional, I would add that vulnerability requires us to covertly (within ourselves) or overtly (with others) express thoughts, feelings, ideas, or desires that are unlikely to be rewarded or valued, either because they are not perceived to match the thoughts, feelings, ideas, or desires of the recipient, or because it will signal that we are different than we have portrayed ourselves to be.

Vulnerability is frequently scary and messy. It amuses me to hear people happily proclaim they are vulnerable and then follow it up by sharing something they are not afraid to expose. It's the equivalent of telling an interviewer that your biggest weakness is that you're a perfectionist. I am terrible at math and it frustrates me, but I could easily stand in front of the world and admit that I have the math skills of a four-year-old. I am also open to admitting that I have cellulite, hate my hair, and wish technology weren't a thing because I struggle with it. Exactly none of that is vulnerability. It was very easy for me to type those words just now without hesitation, and it won't affect me if I am judged for it.

Vulnerability is telling someone that you were molested and raped as a teenager by your father's friend, as an individual shared with me today in an interview for this book. She broke out in hives (I can attest to this as it was a video chat), but she told me anyway.

Vulnerability is pausing but making an attempt to answer questions like, "Do you think you are equipped to run this organization?" as I once asked a male executive coaching client of mine. After a few days he said, "No, I don't. And I struggled with the questions you asked me." That was gold. I knew right away that he would provide an honest, open door into the issues at his company, which was very helpful to me.

People have always told me, "I don't know why I'm telling you this, but… (continues to spill guts)." I take this as a compliment because it means the person feels that I can be trusted not to judge and that I care enough to listen. I would also say it's for a much less honorable reason. I rarely avoid asking a question or making a comment simply because it's uncomfortable (I do try to stop being rude or ignorant). Some of the best conversations I've ever had included a heavy, unexpected, scary dose of vulnerability that resulted in emotional connections I wouldn't ever have experienced if I'd been chatting about the weather or what so-and-so did at work that day. These are the dark caves in which authentic and meaningful relationships are born.

Demonstrating vulnerability with ourselves is one of the hardest things we will ever do. Shattering stories we've told ourselves our whole lives asks us to be honest in a way we can never escape. If you tell your friends you pooped your pants at dinner and they harass you for a year, you can always get new friends. But if you realize you've been giving jurisdiction over your life to someone else because you are fearful, you were manipulated, or you are actually not the confident, capable, talented individual you thought you were, that is something you can't run from. That's scary. It's a dark cave. But it's worth it because then you know how to move forward in life. Even Mario had to fight dragons and fireballs to move to the next level.

This is our Hero's Journey.

When I became vulnerable with myself in my own life, I cried but then stopped almost immediately. I cried again and then stopped abruptly. I thought this was strange until I realized I was watching myself continue to listen to words and phrases that weren't mine:

"Don't be ridiculous."

"Don't be dramatic."

"Everyone else has problems too."

I now recognize these as forms of emotional control in order to make the other person more comfortable. I got very good at not being ridiculous. I am exceptional at controlling my emotions and compartmentalizing them for when I'm alone or for when it's more convenient for everyone else. But I can tell you it has hurt me more than helped me. A fuck I got to drop that day was that I have to be silent and easy regardless of circumstance, meaning logical and controlled at all times.

This is where you get to take your life and break it open.

This is no time to be logical or stifled. This is the *feels* section of the ride.

The moment I realized my first fuck, it sent me into a state of shock. I took four days off work to sit in the first of many breakdowns. In a state of disbelief that I had followed such nonsense for so long, all I could do was sit with my messy parts. There was nowhere else to go. The junk drawers of my soul were flung open. First came anxiety, then sadness, then the good kind of angry.

I like that kind of angry.

If a woman willingly accepts her messy, natural, interesting parts, she deserves a breakdown. Hell, she *needs* a breakdown. Those feelings and fucks need somewhere to go, and I strongly believe in the power of a formal release.

In a few moments, I will help you experience and then release. You are a grown-ass person, and you've lived enough life to have felt what holds you back. You've hung on for this long—maybe because you had to, maybe because you didn't know there was another option, maybe because you needed permission. We've all done it, and there's no judgment in that. But it is natural to feel anger, sadness, chaos, or all of the above. Before moving forward, we will formally work to feel and release that BS energy from your physical and emotional body.

I *love* this part. It is so disruptive and naughty; I was born to enjoy functional rebellion. Maybe you were too.

So let's have a little breakdown, shall we?

During the process of uncovering how you got a little lost in life, a lot comes up. Some of it is absolutely lovely, like realizing how many people have contributed to your well-being and happiness. And some of it is, well, trash. Junk food for the mind, body, and soul. And you may have been eating shit sandwiches for *years*. Most women have lived their entire lives being told to control their emotions. To remain calm and not upset anyone. To avoid coming off "angry" or "bitter," even during outrageously unfair or shocking circumstances.

Fuck. That. Noise.

If you're anything like me, you might go right from seeing your truth to a full breakdown, first curiously uncovering what's been suppressed and then unknowingly boarding the emotional speed train to Whatthefucksville when you realize the extent to which you've been giving others jurisdiction over your life. We all need to feel the weight of our decisions in order for us to truly know that change is necessary, even if it breaks us a little. You have to believe you can withstand temporary pain. As I mentioned previously, avoiding negative or uncomfortable feelings only exacerbates distress. Pulling the wool over your own eyes is easier but not better in the long run.

We all know the catharsis that comes from finally losing our shit (if you don't, I highly recommend it). It's as if you've earned a new level of life, whether it's a renewed feeling of gratitude, a more helpful perspective, or a hard-won rootedness in—and sincere love for—*who you are.*

It's exhausting. It's exhilarating. It's the end of an era.

When women not only find but *feel* clarity and control in their lives, they are unstoppable. They believe anything is possible because it is. All they have to do now is put the pieces back together in a way that represents who they are today. While it's important to notice who you were, who you are, what makes you happy, and what you miss most about yourself, I wholeheartedly believe that moving from noticing to *experiencing* is what makes this process worth going through.

So get angry. Honor resentment. Be sad. Cry. Let go of guilt, and understand that most of the feelings and thoughts you've been avoiding—those things coming back to say, "*Please* pay attention to me!"—have been pushed away because someone else, somehow, in some way, signaled that those things you wanted or those feelings you felt were wrong or open for abandonment. It's a heartbreaking thing to realize that you've neglected your own needs and desires because no one else understood them or validated them. Seeing that you've given away that kind of power is a jagged pill to swallow.

I am now going to ask you to take some time for yourself to release whatever has come up for you. Look over your notes in this book. Count up the number of times a certain name, job, or worry has come up. Consider what has made your heart break a little. Write the biggest fuck you'd like to drop right here:

To honor my life, my soul, and my sanity, I am dropping the belief that:

....

....

....

Then, plan a release.

I call this "smashing the Glass Box." For my entire life I've pic-
tured myself smashing a glass object simply because I didn't
like the way it looked so I could thoughtfully rebuild it in a
way that made it more beautiful to me, and it just stuck. If you
have your own metaphor, use it. The point is, you may need
permission to release everything that has built up, and I'm here
to give it to you.

If you feel fully ready and in a good place, I recommend a few
things depending on circumstances and budget. It could be a
few structured days out of town to reflect on specific behaviors
and patterns or simply an hour to scream, shake, jump, and
cry. One of my favorite breakdowns I got to observe occurred
when two of my best friends called me from outside one of
their houses. One was getting divorced after a sixteen-year
relationship that ended in an affair, and the other was dealing
with the loss of a parent. It was an exceptionally tough year for
them both.

"We're going to break some shit tonight! We wanted to call you!"

They proceeded to smash empty bottles of bourbon against the
brick house. I could hear their wildness among the glass shattering, the freedom that came from saying *fuck it* and enjoying an
unbridled, unfiltered, unencumbered moment together. These
were also two of my most successful and educated friends, which
made their break from propriety that much more amusing.

You've come this far. Make this a special thing you do for yourself. Only you truly know what you need. Oh, and that idea

you're thinking about right now? The thing that precedes the "Yeah, but I can't because…" that's your soul telling you what you need. Do that thing. Or at least write it down and continue to envision it.

I will pause here—mostly for effect, but also because I genuinely want you to put this book down and go find your own version of smashing your Glass Box.

Seriously. Go do it.

SERIOUSLY.

GO DO IT.

So you finally lost your shit. *Good for you!*

Did you smash actual glass? If so, five stars.

Congratulations. *You've just ended the era of your life when you lived according to everyone else.* Honor it, make peace with it, and then look forward to changing the way you show up in the world. If you need to do this a few more times, then do it when you feel the need. Try not to judge your anger, frustration, or anything else. That's slapping your natural, informative emotions in the face.

I did this four times over the span of two years. And truthfully, I'll probably never stop.

Which word resonates most with the feeling you have right now?

- vibrant
- vivacious
- centered
- engaged
- enraged
- powerful
- gorgeous
- glowing
- joyful
- peaceful
- purposeful
- light
- free
- wild

- strong
- driven
- other: choose your own word

Take your word and root into it.

Now that you've physically, emotionally, and mentally expelled negative energy and emotion, you're ready to learn some replacement skills. It's imperative that when we stop engaging in one way of living (i.e., behaving according to what everyone else values or using language that opens doors for criticism) we replace it with something else (i.e., knowing and living via our values or using language that sends new signals).

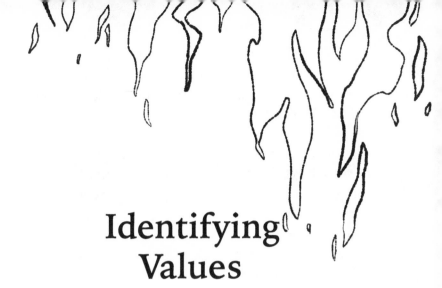

Identifying Values

If you make changes you don't actually care about, they will be unsustainable and you will be miserable.

I'll say it again.

Don't make changes you don't truly care about.

Here I will help you root down in your values.

Rewriting the narrative of your life is hard. Going out into the world as a better version of yourself is one of the most difficult things you'll ever do. But life is designed to reward the resilient and stubborn. You have to naturally care about dropping these beliefs enough to keep going when your spouse doesn't get it, your friends show confusion, your family rolls their eyes, or people try to take you off your game with more of their fucks.

Understanding *why* you want to make this change and how it serves who you are is just as important as picking the fucks you're dropping. It goes against all the work you've done thus far to drop things you think you should, or because your friend did, or because I did. We are all different, and this is not one size fits all. When we know our values, we can root down in our purpose and create a strong foundation for our future.

This is a critical exercise for anyone who is overwhelmed, in need of extra direction, or simply curious about their values. I have made available to readers my BVA (behavioral values assessment) via my website, giannabiscontini.com. It is specifically designed to not only nail down your top five values but to juxtapose your aspirational values (what you want to value or what society tells you you should) and your actual values (where you actually spend your time).

As an example, here are my values:

- creativity
- exploration
- authenticity
- impact
- trust

In every project I take on, in every personal relationship, in every big decision I make, I ensure that at least a few of these are being met or I don't move forward. If any of these are violated, I walk away. This saves me time because I know what's important to me, and I spend little time trying to justify or rationalize working with people who aren't creative, befriending people I don't naturally trust, or taking on work that doesn't allow me to explore, be authentic, or have an impact. It's a simple *no* and then I move on, or an *absolutely* and I move forward. If you can master this, you will spend very little time in limbo.

When you complete the values assessment, fill in the lines below:

- My top three to five values are...

....

....

....

....

....

- Tomorrow, some ways I will officially own and live out my values are...

....

....

....

....

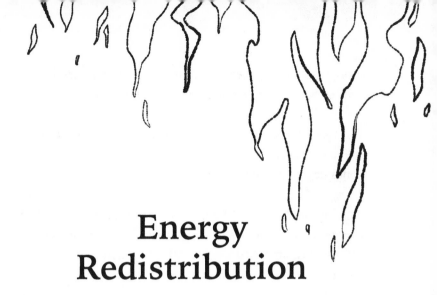

Energy Redistribution

While you're in the process of dropping what doesn't serve you, you may have also realized it's time to redistribute your energy. Now that you've stopped dedicating time to a belief, action, person, or endeavor, to what will you rededicate yourself? Is it something new, or is it spending more time on something or someone you truly care about?

Living on your own terms brings with it a wave of what I can only describe as passionate electricity. I have felt this in my own life, and I've watched other women experience this moment. They're limitless, open, drunk with energy, and unencumbered by the things that no longer fulfill them.

Most importantly, they get the best possible return on their investment. Not money, not fame, not even happiness—they receive *time*. While there will always be only twenty-four hours in a day, women who understand this practice spend their hours more engaged, happier, and more fulfilled than before they learned to increase their awareness and mindful living skills.

This tool is meant to help you understand where you currently spend your energy and will help you stay mindful of where you continue to redistribute it as this work sets in over time.

As with the Behavioral Values Assessment, I've included an energy redistribution chart on giannabiscontini.com, but you can also do a simplified version of this by simply accounting for the hours in your day and noticing in which roles and activities you spend the most time.

After doing so, fill in the lines below:

- I will reduce the time I spend...

....

....

....

- I will spend more time...

....

....

....

Weighing Alternatives

When we decide what to pick up and what to drop in life, it's a big decision that can be quite paralyzing. Choice paralysis is what occurs when there are *too* many choices, and it's shown to decrease the likelihood a decision will be made at all (me in any department store). In modern society, many of us are inundated with a plethora of options that cloud our decision-making skills. While the exercises at the end of each chapter were designed to support you with this, there will always be more choices, questions, and decisions to make about your life, especially in those smaller, day-to-day moments that really count.

To remove much of the mental and emotional labor of making lifestyle choices—from how you eat to where to live to when to change your relationship or job—burn the exercise below into memory.

For most of us, by the time we are compelled to ask ourselves hard questions, staying the course is far scarier than making a change. You've already done this in the previous section, but it's so powerful that I've repeated it here. Use this simple question whenever you are torn on a decision.

Examples:

- What if I stay in this relationship?
- What if I keep talking to myself this way?
- What if I don't take this chance?
- What if I stay in this city?

The possibilities are endless, but the first three words are pure magic. This is a more accurate way of decision-making because you can more reliably predict the outcomes of continuing a behavior or lifestyle rather than the outcomes of doing something new. Facing our own inertia is critical to any evolution.

Try a few "what if" questions and answer in the space below:

....

....

....

....

....

....

Language Signals

How you *talk* about your wants and needs, the language you use to frame the changes you're making and the life you want to lead, is just as important as the alternative decisions you actively make each day. Speaking unapologetically, proudly, and without fucks is critical to maintaining life on your own terms. It lets people know that you are serious and solid. It's important to see the value here.

This skill is meant to help you:

- save energy (instead of inevitably having to defend your new lifestyle choices)
- save time (instead of wasting brain cells thinking of ways to get people off your back, in a nice way)
- protect your changes (instead of backsliding on the changes you know you want and need to make)

For general and fuck-specific language support, you can download a robust PDF guide from giannabiscontini.com.

Please also keep this in mind: *you do not have to explain your choices as much as you think you do.* The simple fact that you have made a choice about your own life is enough.

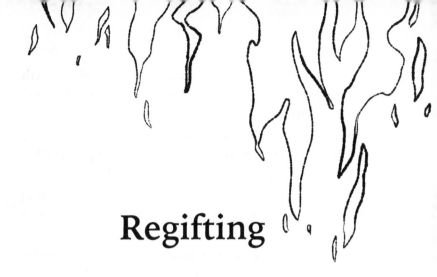

Regifting

This last exercise has helped me fuck-proof my life more than anything I've experienced thus far. When I learned to recognize when I was being given other people's fucks, it was significantly easier to give them back.

Fuck-signaling occurs when we receive signals from others as to what they find valuable or deem "right"—a smile when you mention law school, a frown when you mention becoming a comedian, giggles of delight and approval when you say you're focusing on finding a partner instead of work, or a dismissing shake of the head when you share your dream of traveling the world. People (including you and me) signal their own fucks all the time, and it's important to recognize these moments as thoughts or feelings that belong to the other person. They aren't yours, so give 'em on back. We do this by regifting.

Picture this: A week before your birthday, your best friend calls you and shrieks, "I just got back from vacation, and I have the most amazing present for you!" Your mind buzzes with excitement. Imagining a fine Italian scarf that will perfectly complement your eyes and render the world deeply in love with you, you unwrap the present. *Surprise*, it's a rainbow sequin pashmina. It's the least "you" thing you've ever seen. However, it is very much her style (no judgment—she can pull it off).

The situation feels uncomfortable, but you are clear on your options (because you read this amazing book called *Fuckless*):

- Wear it when you see her and remain horribly uncomfortable in your bedazzled cloak of inauthenticity and awkwardness.
- Kindly give it back, knowing that she'll love it for herself.

Obviously, you give it back kindly, without judgment, and knowing it is very much her, not you. You can give it back without negative results because you know you are coming from a true, authentic place and that cloaking yourself in something that doesn't fit and feels wrong is a crazy waste of time. You have also chosen a best friend who understands, loves, and appreciates you for this ability instead of making you feel small, wrong, or like you have to shut up and wear it because it's her style.

(See what I did there? *Wink.*)

Maybe I'm naive, but I will venture to say that most of the time, when people give you their fucks, it's because they mean well. They think their experience, advice, belief, or story will help you because humans are pretty shitty at taking other people's perspectives. And maybe it *does* help (after all, this book is about teasing out the truths and untruths). But as we've seen, there are many beliefs we want to recreate for ourselves, and that begins with learning to avoid taking on fucks that don't fit in the first place.

Here are some ways you can quickly and easily do this in your life today:

"I can see where you're coming from, but for where I'm going/what I want/what I value, ___ is a better option for me."

"I know you had such a terrible experience with ___, but for me this is the right way to go."

"Thanks so much for the advice. I appreciate it." Then smile and end the conversation.

"Thank you. I appreciate the time you spent thinking about this. It couldn't have been easy to share your opinion with me." Did you know you don't actually have to explain yourself or your choices? You can just love people for caring!

Now we will focus on a few other actions you can take to wrap up your *Fuckless* journey. The oh-so-important cherry on top of all the work you've done thus far.

Create the
Open Door

During my graduate school's commencement speech, the speaker praised us for our hard work at the academically rigorous and prestigious university. She told us about all the doors we opened for ourselves by pursuing an advanced degree and filled us with hope for our future. Then she said the following—it was simple but stuck with me for the next thirteen years:

"And when you walk through the door of opportunity, turn around and take someone with you."

As a behavior analyst, I'm grateful to have a behind-the-curtain understanding of how humans work. The world doesn't behave; people do. Groups don't behave; individuals do. And people watch other people behave. They observe the consequences of other people's behavior, good or bad, which creates a learning history (the corporate world likes to call this "culture"). By changing your behavior, you change the behavior of the people around you—your kids, your friends, your partner, your coworkers, your boss, the cashier at the grocery store. You get to set different rules for how things go with you, different rules for what you want, what you need, and what controls you. You send new signals for who you are and the life you want, what you accept and what you don't.

How refreshing is that?

It's easy to look at this giant, frustrating, patriarchal society and shrug our shoulders. It's easy to blame men or our parents or institutional sexism for a number of things. And believe me, I'm not saying those things don't exist or don't matter. I'm saying they need you in order to continue along the positive trajectory progressive people of all genders have been pushing for over a century.

We live in a world that continues to rally against women who stand taller. That doesn't mean that people are evil and want to see women fail. It means that smart women ask questions. Purpose-driven women move mountains. *Fuckless* women are unaffected by anything that exists to derail them. The woman who decides to challenge the rules that have shaped her is a threat to the storyline. A beautiful, powerful, game-changing threat. And supporting other women who decide to first challenge and re-create their own stories is how we sustainably change the world.

Whoever is popping up in your mind right now, whoever might appreciate or want to learn more about these concepts or this work, consider how you might be a catalyst for change in their life. Maybe it's (tactfully!) giving them this book. Maybe it's sharing pieces of your own journey. Or maybe it's just listening while they make their own way to their own change and being there for encouragement once they decide.

Celebrate

You've evaluated all the fucks you've been given. You've chosen the ones to drop. You've braved the uncomfortable feelings about where they came from and why you held on for so long. Maybe you cried. Maybe you had an epic, freeing breakdown. Maybe you broke some shit.

It would be the honor of my life to know this book gifted you with the naughty exhilaration of doing so.

So I would like to take a moment to celebrate *you*.

From my heart to yours, well done. I know the process of getting here was more arduous and awkward than you would have liked, but in exchange, you've got more self-awareness, more self-love, and the ability to recalibrate. With these skills, you can now live your life from the inside. No one gets the gift of rewriting their beliefs without eating a few shit nuggets.

Thank you for eating shit nuggets to elevate your life and send yourself back out into the world, battered, bruised, and fucking beautiful. After finishing this chapter, please do something incredible for yourself. Something *all you*. I recommend time alone or with your most supportive friends or family, with something delicious, in a beautiful, quiet setting you've never been to before (even if it's just walking down a random street).

Go On, *Glow*

When we disrupt false beliefs, we are free to create our own, *more functional* truth instead. Seeing pieces of my life and of the world for what they truly are changed what they looked like. Beliefs and tangibles I placed worth upon no longer held value. There were things I couldn't unsee, and there were many fucks that were easy to walk away from. Still, I'm a work in progress, and you will be too.

My favorite comment I continue to receive as a coach is that I wouldn't ask clients to do anything I wouldn't do or haven't done in my own life. The exercises in this book are how I survived and grew from an unthinkably dark two years of my life, improved for your experience. I've shared a lot of my messiness with you already, but I would be remiss not to also share the actual results of my own process.

When I dropped Being Small:

- I rediscovered my love for food.
- My mind and my body became vessels for action and positive change, not shame, guilt, or passivity.
- I developed an overt confidence for my voice, opinions, and ideas.
- My "extra" became a positive, glowing differentiator.
- I regained energy and brainpower once reserved for overthinking and forcing myself to be small.

When I dropped Being Soft:

- My definition of strength became "vulnerability, patience, and grace."
- I became a better mom to my rescue pups.
- I developed an integrated physical and mental ritual to put me in a place of power whenever I needed it.
- I became a ninja at speaking up against injustices wherever I saw them.

When I dropped Being Less:

- I wrote this book.
- I began formally working to elevate and advance women at home, at work, and in society.
- I stopped hesitating to take what I wanted at work and in life.

When I dropped Being the Exception:

- I stopped using gender qualifiers altogether, or solely for women.

- I tasked myself with living by example, wherever I could, for any young girls who might be watching.
- I approached more "out of reach" business opportunities.

When I dropped Being Stifled:

- I recognized my emotions as critical signals and divine feminine knowledge.
- I became more aware of my emotion-body connection and developed a shake-dance-cry practice to distribute negative energy and evoke a sense of freedom.
- I attracted people who appreciate me for my range—from my "extra" to my depression—and created space from those who didn't, giving me added feelings of belonging and acceptance.

When I dropped Being Everything:

- I said no to things that did not contribute to my life, creating dozens of hours a month to reengage in work and social activities that added to my growth and new lifestyle.
- I evaluated all relationships and created space where needed, giving me more energy and emotional freedom.
- I found the time and energy to write this book.

When I dropped Being Chosen:

- I left my marriage.
- I felt powerful and genuinely enough just as I am.
- I became a deeper, more complex, more interesting version of myself.
- I had more time to focus on my desires, my work, and my lifestyle.

When I dropped Being Dependent:

- I took greater control over my finances.
- I bought and restored a 1931 vintage cottage three thousand miles from my current home.
- I became savage in rebuilding and positioning my work as a main priority.
- I started solo road tripping around the West, exploring places I'd always wanted to see.

When I dropped Being Fixed:

- I made investments in products and experiences that truly elevated me and contributed to my happiness and well-being.
- I gained a new level of self-acceptance and peace.
- I reduced time on social media because I viewed it as an instigator to lowering my mood while increasing my buying and feelings of scarcity.

When I dropped Being Sexy...But Sweet:

- My attire became less about my sexuality or gender and more about my mood, including men's or gender-ambiguous clothing.
- I created space from people who overfocused on my physical appearance.
- I realized the sexual identity and desires unique to me were open for experimentation.
- I opened myself to other genders and had lovely, exploratory adventures with couples.
- I updated my definition of sexy to include:

- Natural
- Intelligent
- Untamed hair
- "Zero-effort outfits" (clothes that did not cause stress but joy when putting them together).

I so look forward to hearing your journeys, struggles, and successes along the way.

If you feel compelled to share your story, please send me a DM or reach out through my Instagram page @giannabiscontini.

I hope this list inspires you and shows you what is possible, but I'll drop a word of caution here. This book is not about perfection, how I've grown, or how the people around you are growing—it's about *you*. Messy, beautiful, cracked, glowing you. I am still a work in progress and could write many more books about the things I still get wrong. Elevating our lives and living on our terms is not about buffing out imperfections until we're the perfect version of ourselves; it's about looking at those cracks and heartache and mistakes and honoring them as the unique, interesting story of *you*.

"How do I do this?" you might ask. You bring a little *wabi-sabi* into your life.

In Japanese culture, the concept of beauty is very different from what most of us in the West have been conditioned to aspire to. *Wabi-sabi* is defined as "a worldview centered on the acceptance of transience and imperfection. The aesthetic is sometimes described as one of appreciating beauty that is 'imperfect, impermanent, and incomplete' in nature."

This concept is brought to life in the art of *kintsugi*, meaning "golden joinery." Long ago, when pottery cracked or broke, it would not be thrown away but instead joined back together with lacquer dusted or mixed with gold powder. This honors and highlights breakage and cracks in the object as part of its history, instead of something to disguise or toss aside. Japanese aesthetics actually values marks of wear and tear from years of use.

Take a deep breath, and look at your body. Look down at your arms and legs. Pull your shirt up and look at your belly. Maybe look in the mirror at your face.

Now picture every mistake, every regret, every hard thing you learned or remembered while reading this book, and draw with your mind a gold crack somewhere on your skin. Spend a few moments touching the gold cracks, recalling what you learned or how you grew, or simply admiring them.

Think of the Glass Box you lived in and eventually smashed. Can you put it back together with gold and admire it now that you no longer live there?

A *Fuckless* female is gloriously unaffected; her self-worth and identity no longer depend on those around her. She no longer lives in a polarizing, confusing whirlwind of other people's ideas and beliefs. She no longer spends her time focused on what everyone else thinks she should do, wear, eat, or say. She no longer lives to be liked. She no longer has the compulsion to halt her life in order to get permission. For anything.

She is light and happy, grounded and solid, poised AF. She

inspires change in those around her simply by living her life in a way that shows her truth. She radiates and glows and draws people in with her vivacious, vibrant "ness." She honors with grace the years she gave the world jurisdiction over her life, because she knows she couldn't have gotten to this place without doing it everyone else's way first. There is only one person left to live for.

She Fucks Like a Goddess. She is Untamed. She Buys Herself the Fucking Lilies. She says Fuck No to shit she doesn't want to do. She thinks We Should All Be Feminists. She surrounds herself with books, songs, art, and people who get this life she's building. She is a free, wild being, capable of not only running her own life but owning it so hard that she one day realizes she's changed her entire world.

Now more than ever, the world needs more women like her. Like *you*.

Positive change is not leaps and bounds but small, seemingly insignificant steps each day to modify how we live by sending behavioral signals regarding the lives we lead, what we tolerate, and what we stand for. Positive change is not excuses and blame, but a choice we make to walk our own talk and live *our* lives on *our* terms.

That, my friend, is true power. And your power does not exist in a vacuum. It is contagious. It is infinite. It raises us all.

Reinforcement and Punishment

Reinforcement simply means "anything that is added to or subtracted from the environment that *increases* the likelihood a given behavior will occur in the future, under similar conditions." Reinforcement can be positive or negative, meaning *added to or subtracted from*, not whether it is "good" or "bad." This differs from punishment only in that punishment means "anything added to or subtracted from the environment that *reduces* the likelihood a given behavior will occur in the future under similar conditions." Punishment can also be positive (if something is added) or negative (if something is removed).

Very simple examples:

- *Positive reinforcement*: Jill takes out the trash, and Jack gives Jill something she wants/likes. Jill now takes out the trash every week.
- *Negative reinforcement*: Jill takes out the trash, and Jack says,

"Thanks for doing that. I'll take the laundry off your plate for you." Jill continues to take out the trash.

- *Positive punishment*: Jill takes out the trash. Jack says, "It's about fucking time," and adds "trash" to her chore list. Jill stops taking out the trash.
- *Negative punishment*: Jill takes out the trash, and Jack says, "I don't want you taking out the trash! If you do that again, I won't do that thing you like." Jill stops taking out the trash.

When people say reinforcement doesn't work (and there are very influential professionals who do so), what they actually mean is that what was used in an *attempt* to make a behavior happen again failed to work. If it does not successfully increase the likelihood of future behavior, it is, by definition, not reinforcement. There are people who will say that punishment also does not work. This isn't necessarily true. Punishment works if it reduces a behavior, period. But it's also very shortsighted. Research shows that reinforcement is more sustainable and preferred in most cases, like rewarding someone for eating healthy food instead of shaming them for eating unhealthy food. Both work, but one is preferable.

A common example I hear in meetings with my culture analytics clients:

"I know we are supposed to be rewarding employees, but we've tried that. We gave bonuses based on performance, and it didn't work. Reward systems are ineffective, and our people are lazy."

Giving people more money is a successful reinforcement strategy *if* it results in them performing better, but if they fail to improve their performance after being provided extra money, it is not reinforcement. Maybe employees want to perform better but don't know how (skill deficit). Maybe the amount of money isn't enough for the amount of time and effort required (performance deficit or low reward for high response effort). Maybe they have the financial resources they need, and money is not valuable enough, but time off might be. In this case, a *negative* reinforcement strategy would be more effective. Instead of giving employees *more* of something (positive reinforcement) they could *remove* something aversive (work). If employees earn extra PTO for a specific behavior or performance and performance improves, we can call this successful negative reinforcement. In my own work I have seen great improvements in performance when employees are able to delegate or offload soul-crushing administrative tasks.

The annoying thing about reinforcement is you've got to stay on top of it and measure it so you know it's continuously working for everyone. When it stops being effective, it is called satiation or possibly habituation, depending on the circumstance. Time to analyze reinforcement preferences again. Reward systems are complicated and involve changing variables that can be hard to stay on top of, which is why I have a job.

REINFORCEMENT SCHEDULES

In addition to assessing whether positive and negative reinforcement or positive and negative punishment is at play, we also analyze how reinforcement or punishment is provided in regard to timing and frequency.

Schedules of reinforcement operate according to ratios or intervals and are fixed or variable. These are extremely complicated and go beyond the scope of this appendix. But here's a little tidbit for those interested.

For example, a FR1 (fixed ratio of 1) schedule of reinforcement simply means that for every response there will be a reward. An FR3 schedule would mean that a reward is given after every third time a behavior occurs. Why does this matter? If you've ever sat at a slot machine, you're probably on a *variable* ratio (VR400) schedule, meaning that about every four hundredth time the slot is pulled a reward is given, give or take a few dozen or so. This is called intermittent reinforcement and is the most effective way to get someone to keep engaging in a desired behavior.

THE FOUR FUNCTIONS AND FUNCTIONALLY EQUIVALENT REPLACEMENT BEHAVIOR (FERB)

There are four categories of reasons we do anything:

1. Attention
2. Escape/avoidance
3. Access to tangible items
4. Automatic (Some call it "intrinsic" or "sensory." This type is not dependent on anyone else or what we call "socially mediated.")

We very often draw quick conclusions about why someone is doing something because our brains like fast answers that make sense to us, but behavior is actually quite complicated. One can engage in the same behavior for each of all four reasons.

I like to use sticky examples so people remember things:

- You masturbate because your partner thinks it's hot: access to attention.
- You masturbate because it's either that or the dishes: escape/avoidance.
- You masturbate because someone pays you: access to a tangible item.
- You masturbate because it is physically satisfying: automatic.

Knowing *why* we do something is important because if we want to stop doing it, we have to replace it with a FERB. We have to figure out what we are getting from that activity or behavior (one of the four categories) so we can replace that activity with something that gets us the same result. This is why many self-help strategies are tragically unhelpful and oversimplified. Telling someone what to eat and how to exercise fails to take into account why they are *not* currently doing so. Most of us know how to lose weight; we just can't bring ourselves to engage in the behavior daily for a variety of reasons. Mostly, it takes a lot of energy and change (high response effort) and takes a long time to see results (latency between behavior and result is long).

We likely don't need more education on healthy living; we need less stress and more energy (changes in the environment around us) to make these healthy behaviors more likely to happen.

DEPRIVATION AND SATIATION

This is a simple concept but, like most things in science, also complex. In regard to the value of anything—be it an item, someone's attention, or a feeling—the less we have it, the more valuable it becomes. Conversely, the more of it we have, the less valuable it becomes.

My favorite example from my own life is my trick to stop myself from blowing money on clothes whenever I am bored with my closet. I regularly take half of the clothes in my closet and put them away (deprivation) for a month or so. This increases their value, and when I change closets each four to eight weeks, the clothes feel "new" to me. Have you ever found a dress or pair of shoes in the back of your closet and thought, *Oh my gosh, I love these! Why don't I wear them more often?* That's deprivation at play. At one time you probably loved them just the same but became habituated to them. Habituation simply means you become used to something, and it no longer has the same effect. We can also become satiated on attention, a feeling, or an item, meaning that we no longer want it or will engage in a specific behavior to gain it. My favorite example here is dessert. I used to treat myself to dessert after completing a certain number of work tasks or long runs. As it turns out, I can only handle so much sugar. Eventually, you couldn't have paid me to eat dessert (and in that case, dessert could be used for punishment—ha).

It's not that I never wanted dessert again. I simply needed to adjust my reinforcement schedule or type of reward (a candle instead of cake, ten runs instead of five, etc.) to increase the value of dessert, even if it was just telling myself, "No dessert for three months." Even the thought of being deprived can increase the value of something! The lack of understanding of deprivation and satiation, in addition to reinforcement schedules, is why many people roll their eyes at the word *reward* or *reinforcement*, considering it academic or outdated jibber jabber.

Many of the concepts discussed here and throughout the book may feel reductionist or oversimplified. However, behavior is extremely well researched on our end, and we know it is more complex than I quickly outlined above. It is my hope that with an increased understanding and utilization of true behavior science, we can change the world in big ways at the speed we must do so to preserve the planet, improve human rights, and improve our global political climate. I believe in humanity, and I will keep this hope with me for the rest of my days.

9 781544 530468